Praise for

Vicki Hoefle

Duct Tape Parenting

"Parenting books are like diet books: They work for a while and then you're back to blimpdom. *Duct Tape Parenting* seems like something else—an idea that's workable for the long run, because, at base, it believes in the kids themselves."
—Lenore Skenazy, founder of the book and blog, *Free-Range Kids*

"*Duct Tape Parenting* is for every parent who's grown tired of picking up after the kids, taming sibling squabbles, and doing all the work around the house. In an age of overly involved parents, Vicki Hoefle offers a battle cry of sanity. I read her book in one weekend, immediately put her wisdom to use, and saw results right away. I was stunned. If you want to change the dynamic in your household and nurture self-reliant, thoughtful, and resilient children, read this book."
—Katherine Ozment, contributing editor and weekly columnist for *Boston Magazine*

"Vicki Hoefle does an amazing job in *Duct Tape Parenting* of providing relatable, helpful advice. Her approach is unique and extremely thought provoking. This is a must-read for parents who are tired of advice that does not work and need a re-charge for their families."
—Vanessa Van Petten, author, RadicalParenting.com

"In this gem of a book, Vicki Hoefle gives parents a common-sense approach to raising respectful, responsible, and resilient children. Her lighthearted, down-to-earth manner helps parents clarify their goals for their families, understand the roots of behavior, and develop a path to creating a happy, healthy, and supportive family life."
—Amy Lew, PhD, author of *Raising Kids Who Can*

"The most important family dynamic that we have achieved as a result of Vicki Hoefle's approach is one of mutual respect. We feel like a team, like four people who can depend upon each other. This book is a must-read for any family who is looking to create a supportive unit built on honesty and trust."
—Katy Smith Abbott, Dean of Students and Assistant Professor of the History of Art and Architecture, Middlebury College

"An informative and irreverent guide, this book is a must-read for anyone who wants to raise resilient, problem-solving children. Vicki Hoefle offers a Goldilocks way forward: not too much parenting, not too little, just right."
—Craig Idlebrook, writer and parent-educator with the Boot Camp for New Dads Project. www.bootcampfordads.org

"If you are interested in more positive family relationships and raising capable children who will courageously step into adulthood, take the opportunity to read this book. It is never too late to change your life."
—Cindy Pierce, mother, innkeeper, comic, author of *Finding the Doorbell, Sexual Satisfaction for the Long Haul*

"This is a must-read for every parent, parent educator, and teacher. The exercises help you identify the problem and the little reminders tell you exactly what to do—'putting on the duct tape'—when to do, and why to do. As a counselor and educator, I recommend this book wholeheartedly to every parent and any individual who works with children. The ideas are so applicable, that I will use some of them in my classes, even at the graduate level! And as a parent my duct tape is ready...finally."
—Bengu Erguner-Tekinalp, PhD, Assistant Professor, Counselor Education, Drake University

"Rarely does a book come along that offers parents solid information about why a parenting style is so important, tools and tips that make it easy to try, and inspiration that keeps us afloat as we find our way. Vicki Hoefle is the real deal. She's parented five kids and taught thousands of parents with this approach. This book should definitely be on the top of your stack!"
—Dina Emser, Certified Positive Discipline Lead Trainer, author of *Roadmap to Success* and *Trusting the Fortune Within*

"Hoefle's straightforward approach to empowering our children debunks the parenting myths that often cause unnecessary stressors that are all too common within families. Her techniques and highly identifiable case studies demonstrate that it is possible for parents to have mutually respectful relationships with their children, while lovingly engaging with them and providing the knowledge that builds their abilities, confidence, and independence."
—Dawn Lyons, freelance writer and editor, teen consultant and advocate, www.linesbylyons.com

Duct Tape Parenting

Duct Tape Parenting

A LESS IS MORE APPROACH
TO RAISING RESPECTFUL,
RESPONSIBLE, & RESILIENT KIDS

Vicki Hoefle

First published by Bibliomotion ,Inc.
33 Manchester Road
Brookline, MA 02446
Tel: 617- 934- 2427
www.bibliomotion.com

Printed in the United States of America

Library of Congress Cataloging-in-Publication Data

Hoefle, Vicki.
    Duct tape parenting : a less is more approach to raising respectful,
responsible, and resilient kids / Vicki Hoefle.
       p. cm.
    ISBN 978-1-937134-18-1 (pbk. : alk. paper)
    1. Parenting.   2. Child rearing.   I. Title.
    HQ755.8.H588 2012
    649'.1—dc23
                                                    2012025600

For my husband, Iain, and children,
Hannah, Colin, Zoe, Kiera, Brady and Michael,
Brie and Mason.

CONTENTS

FOREWORD

It's a lot easier teaching other people's kids than parenting my own.

And while teaching has brought me five minutes of fame on *The CBS Evening News* with Katie Couric and to the White House Rose Garden to meet the President and First Lady, parenting has offered me no such accolades or acclaim. Sure, the hugs from my kids and seeing their progress in life are great intrinsic rewards, but a whole lot of parenting, for me, has at times felt really thankless and downright hard.

I admit it, when we had our first child, I had never so much as held a newborn before. I had no clue. And while in other parts of my life I had ample training—for my teaching I had years of classes, student teaching, and professional development, and for my competitive swimming there were lessons, teams, and coaches showing me the way—for parenting I felt like I had been thrown into the deep end of the pool, not knowing how to even tread water.

Now, in my mind, my wife Megan must have had it all figured out. She is naturally nurturing, has a close relationship with her own parents, had held and even babysat kids for years. When we had baby number one, Megan was reading lots of parenting books, sharing what she was learning with me over scattered dinners as we switched off holding and bouncing this squirmy being who did not seem to prefer a quiet and leisurely meal.

And, yet, one day we found ourselves on the landing of our townhouse stairway, the first baby now a three-year-old who had been out of sorts since our second child was born a few months earlier. Said three-year-old was screaming from the downstairs bathroom for her mom to come wipe her bottom, which we knew full well she was capable of doing herself. Megan tried to tell her such, which only escalated her screaming, whining and demanding of her mother's help and full attention, *now*, no matter that (or perhaps because) the baby was also crying and needing attention from his mom.

Then, my usually poised and confident wife, with figurative steam coming out of her ears, melted down, right there on the stairway landing. After a few unmentionable words under her breath, she said, "That's it. I give up. I am contacting Vicki Hoefle, NOW!"

Megan had heard about Vicki Hoefle and her program from a colleague, had been looking at Vicki's website and liked what she was reading. So, that fateful day, Megan wrote an e-mail to Vicki, explaining the bottom-wiping situation, and telling her, "I have half a PhD and, in this seemingly simple, everyday situation, I have absolutely no clue what to do." Our relationship with Vicki was born that day, and we haven't looked back.

I often wonder: Why is it that we think we need training for our careers, our sports, so many things we do in life—but not parenting? Especially, us educators and educated folks. We somehow think we should just know how to be great parents. Many of us are too proud to admit that we need some training to be the kind of parents we want to be. That effective (meaning, to me, empowering, peaceful) parenting is not necessarily just instinctual—well, at least not in today's modern culture where our biological and spiritual instincts are layered over with centuries of media talk, cultural talk, and downright toxic talk.

Vicki's approach is not just her harebrained notions about what makes a good parent—it is based on the well-respected and well-researched work of psychologists Dr. Alfred Adler and Dr. Rudolf Dreikurs. Vicki discovered Adler's work—often called "individual psychology" and based on the optimistic concept that people can be well-adjusted, happy, and contributing members of society (as opposed to the darker, Freudian psychoanalytic view of the human condition)—early on in her parenting career. She used it as the basis of her work as a preschool director, and as the mother of five, herself. She used Adler's philosophy, the child—and family—centered work of Adler's protégé Dreikurs, and the work of other Adlerian colleagues, to create her comprehensive parenting program for the masses.

One of the things that sold us on Vicki is that she tells you up front that it is going to take years of hard work to create the family of your dreams—it can be fun, but it will not be quick and easy. This is not a quick-fix; it is a commitment to self-examination, to assuming responsibility, to evolving, and to taking risks—and it is a life-long commitment. "Go slow," she always says.

While this may sound overwhelming to some who are seeking the crash course in perfect parenting, to me, it is the ultimate reason to consider this approach: it is real. And real is what I am all about as a teacher, a person, and as a family man. I know, from my career, from my sports, from my life, that achieving our goals is a never-ending process, which does not happen overnight, and that we need all the enlightened trainers we can get to support us in our journeys.

The other thing that led us to put our trust in Vicki is that she shares a core philosophy with me, as a teacher and father, and my wife: Vicki respects children. Her program is based on respecting children, listening to them, and working with them—not doing to them or for them, but collaborating together with them, as members of a family, so we all grow. This is how I teach my students, and how I want to raise my kids.

This—I know for sure—is how kids learn to respect themselves and others. Not by being "shown who's boss" or by being given everything they ask for, but by being included in the real conversations and problem-solving, offered a true role, allowed to make their own choices and experience the results. I've been called "unconventional" as a teacher because I deal with kids this way; Vicki has been called the same as a parent educator. But I think she and I can both attest to the reality that kids absolutely and unequivocally thrive when they are given true respect and the opportunity to engage in their own lives.

Vicki trains parents the way I train teachers—by showing them the mirror. If your kids are misbehaving, we say, look at your own behavior first. This is not to blame, but to empower. It is only by empowering the teachers (the parents) to analyze and change their own words and actions that we can ever see change in the words and actions of the children in their charge. We can only teach responsibility by taking it ourselves. Vicki gets this, to the core, and it is the heart of approach.

Vicki Hoefle is as enlightened a trainer as I have come across, in my acclaimed career as a Teacher of the Year, and in my oh-so-humble occupation as a father and husband. And this approach offers any family a grounded philosophy, structure, and training toolbox—based on the highest of values of love, respect, and empowerment—that I could not recommend more highly.

There are still many days that I find teaching math to my dozens of at-risk, middle school students easier than parenting my own two small children. But, now I at least feel that I have my head above water as a father, I have a great coach, and I am learning the strokes it will take to get my family and me triumphantly to the finish line.

Alex Kajitani
California Teacher of the Year, 2009
Top-4 Finalist, National Teacher of the Year, 2009

ACKNOWLEDGMENTS

I want to thank everyone who has ever been a part of my life, because without them I would not be the person I am today. A special thanks to my husband and children who, it goes without saying, are the light of my life.

Thank you to all the parents who have participated in my classes over the last twenty years and urged me to write a book that they could recommend to family and friends around the world. Thank you to all the parents who generously shared their stories to be included as illustration of the concepts in this book.

I would like to give a special thank you to Dr. Alfred Adler, Dr. Rudolf Dreikurs, and the entire Adlerian Community. None of this information is my creation. I am only the messenger who has offered her interpretation of their research.

Thank you to the amazing group of individuals who supported this project: Therese Fafard and Nathan Heilman for their never-ending support and the introduction to the Bibliomotion team; everyone at Bibliomotion who has been right there with us, every step of the way; Jamaica Jenkins for her enthusiasm, energy, and her ability to capture my snarky voice in a way that translates on paper; and to my colleague, business partner, and best friend, Jennifer Nault who encouraged and supported me throughout this project.

Finally, thank you to every parent, every child, and every family that is committed to creating healthy, loving relationships.

INTRODUCTION

Twenty years ago, when I set off on my own parenting adventure, I knew I wanted to create a strong bond with my children, I wanted to be a loving mother, and I wanted to live a balanced, happy life, all while preparing my kids for the real world. I was lucky enough to pick up *The Parent's Handbook: Systematic Training for Effective Parenting* by Don Dinkmeyer Sr., Gary McKay, and Don Dinkmeyer Jr. before my daughter was even born.

This book introduced me to the work of Dr. Alfred Adler and Dr. Rudolf Dreikurs, both of whom were influential in helping parents raise children in a respectful, cooperative, and democratic environment. Of all the ideas, concepts, and techniques I was introduced to, what resonated most for me were these two beliefs: a misbehaving child is a discouraged child and it is the parents' responsibility to prepare their children to become contributing members of society. With those two ideas in mind and a voracious appetite to learn all I could about individual psychology, I set about the task of becoming informed on how to raise thinking, engaged, cooperative, empowered children. I read, studied, attended conferences, and put into practice everything I was learning about the parent/child relationship.

After my daughter was born, I made the decision to leave corporate America and stay home with her. The only problem was, I needed to make money. I decided that, since I was having such a great time raising my own child, I would start a small, in-home daycare and introduce parents to the philosophy I was using with my own children by teaching an informal six-week class.

As time went on, the center grew to include more than thirty children and five full-time staff members, and I continued teaching the parenting classes to bigger groups. I had two more children and, shortly after my third child was born, I decided to retire and move to the East Coast, where I could raise the kids in a rural setting with room to roam. It wasn't long before I was leading parenting classes again, and I have been teaching ever since.

When asked why, after twenty years of teaching, I am still as enthusiastic and excited about presenting this material; my answer is always the same.

I teach for two reasons. The first is that this approach to raising children works. It worked for me as a new mother juggling three children and a new career. It worked when I became a single mother of three still working in her career of choice, although it barely paid the bills. It worked when I met the man I would later marry, who had a very different approach to parenting and two children who had lost their mom when they were young. It worked as we combined our families and it continued to work as our children grew into adolescents and then into young adults. This approach works for my family as a whole and for each of us as individuals.

And I teach because this approach to parenting works for other families. If it didn't, I would be out of business. For most of my career, the only advertising I did was by word of mouth. Never, in twenty years of teaching, has one of my classes gone unfilled—in fact, they tend to be booked at least six months in advance. Something is working. I don't always know what that something is, but there is magic in this approach to parenting and it is my honor to share it with parents who yearn for a deeper, more meaningful and more enjoyable life with kids.

Thanks to my background in Adlerian psychology and a commitment to this philosophy; a suite of tools that works whether kids are aged two, five, nine, fifteen, or twenty-two; commonsense solutions that address everything from morning chaos, bedtime meltdown, sibling squabbles, and snarky attitudes; and duct tape, my constant companion, I guided my family while keeping a very different frame of mind than most of the parents I knew around town. It was not uncommon for people to ask me, with five children in tow, *How do you do it?*

And my answer was always the same, "With a supply of duct tape to help me manage my mouth, controlling ways, and dictating tendencies and a commonsense approach for raising kids who will one day leave my home and live their lives without my supervision." Like any family, we had ups and downs, but what I developed over time was a clear and sustainable approach to parenting.

Duct Tape Parenting is a hands-off approach to parenting with a focus on developing and deepening the relationship between parents and kids without anyone feeling like a doormat or a dictator. Duct Tape Parenting is meant for the long haul.

Over the years, I have learned a few things about parents and their need for a "quick-fix" solution to a behavior problem. I also recognized that the parenting advice industry is all too willing to provide these "quick fixes" to bring temporary relief to concerned parents who are desperate to bring peace and calm back into their lives.

Duct Tape Parenting doesn't offer quick fixes. It is my

belief that until parents understand exactly what is going on in their homes, realize the part they play in both the challenges and successes of the family, and see how their children respond when they are not being micromanaged by their parents, nothing is likely to change for more than a week or two. But because parents often reach for a parenting book when they are feeling vulnerable and frustrated, they succumb to a "quick-fix" strategy that, in the end, further alienates their children and leaves them feeling even more discouraged. As the mother of five and a professional parent educator, I cannot, in good conscience, offer solutions that I know won't bring the lasting change that parents are truly looking for. This approach to parenting, with its focus on progress and improvement and on the idea that change happens over time, is for parents willing to put the work into the most important relationship they will have—the one with their child.

In the first section of this book, we'll identify some of the biggest obstacles we face as parents and begin to recognize how we can clear away what is *not* working. In the second section of the book, we'll replace what's not working with information and tips that *do work* and that will set you on a new road with your family. There isn't a one-size-fits-all magic solution that will lead you into bliss *but* there is a one-sized-feels-awesome-for-all outcome: a happy, stable family with children who can think for themselves and parents who can turn the lights out at the end of the day and say, *I feel good about where we're headed.* We all deserve to feel confident in our parenting, to enjoy our children, and to prepare our children to live happy and fulfilling lives, and that's why this book was written. To help you, no matter where you are in your journey, get back on track and make the changes you need for an enjoyable family experience.

SECTION I

BEFORE WE GET THE DUCT TAPE, LET'S SEE WHAT NEEDS FIXING: NOTE, IT'S *NOT* THE KIDS

Let's face it, parenting is challenging even on a good day. In my experience as both a mom and a professional parent educator with more than twenty years in the trenches, I believe parents are doing the best they can with the information they have. And that's part of the problem. The information they currently have and the information they use to make the majority of their parenting decisions is based on a question I am asked a dozen times a day: "How do I get my kids to start doing this/stop doing that?" Parents across the country mistakenly believe that finding a strategy to "get" the kids to do or not do something is where they ought to be spending their time, energy, and money.

The problem is that the majority of the strategies parents employ to wrangle their kids into behaving don't make things better for more than a day or two, which sends parents back out to find yet another "quick-fix" behavior strategy. Parents struggle to understand why the advice they received from a trusted friend, the article they saw on the Internet, the program with sensational testimonials, or the book they have read four times and highlighted until it glows in fluorescent yellow doesn't deliver the kind of lasting and substantial change they are looking for.

New information and a new way of thinking are required if parents are to experience deep and lasting change. In this section, I will share five of the most common mistakes parents make and how a small shift in thinking, coupled with new information, can and will dramatically impact you, your kids, and the family as a whole.

1

Feeding the Weed:
Your Focus Is the Problem

The key to success is to focus our conscious mind on things we desire not things we fear.

—Brian Tracy

You get more of what you pay attention to.

—Vicki Hoefle

In my parenting course, I introduce a provocative, and powerful exercise to help parents understand the connection between their child's behavior, the strategies parents use to deal with this behavior, and how the interaction may be making things worse, not better.

I ask the parents in the audience to shout out all the annoying, aggravating, and maddening behaviors their children exhibit on any given day while I capture them on the left side of a large, blank piece of paper. The goal here is to encourage parents to open up and admit that they do indeed carry around a list of behaviors their children exhibit, which they are working furiously to get rid of. By doing this as a group, parents also feel relieved to see they are not alone.

Sometimes, the list bursts onto the board and within a few minutes we easily have twenty to thirty behaviors lined up next to each other. (You'll see examples later in this chapter.) Other times, the class is more cautious and reserved, and it takes a bit of prodding before they open up and start slinging the truth my way. Either way, we eventually get to a hearty bunch of verbs that make parents cringe, nod, shake their heads, and give an "amen" in agreement.

Next to the list of problematic behaviors, I draw a very small weed winding its way from the bottom of the list all the way to the top. I ask the parents to visualize each of these pesky behaviors (even the ones they really, really can't stand) as simply small, budding weeds that, initially, are nothing to be alarmed about.

I then ask the parents to shout out all the strategies, techniques, and tools they employ to deal with these problematic behaviors. Again, I write down everything they throw my way, recording them on the other side of the paper (you'll see examples later in this chapter). To get to the point of the exercise, I say: "If the behaviors you listed on the left side of the paper are the weeds, make a guess and tell me what you think the list on the right side of the paper with all those strategies, techniques, and tools you are currently using might be considered."

There is a pause and then, without warning, a parent invariably shouts out, "The fertilizer?"

Exactly: all those so-called parenting strategies you are currently using to deal with the list of pesky behaviors are the fertilizer. And then I help them anchor the connection: "Parents, your attention—whether it's good, bad, unintentional, unnoticed, unplanned, reflexive, angry, sugarcoated, sincere, or otherwise—is the fertilizer that makes it possible for those weeds to grab hold, grow roots, and take over the family. The behaviors can't grow without your tending to them on a regular and consistent basis. As well-meaning parents, you care for the very weed you cannot stand."

I know this may sound counterintuitive to your role as a parent, and that is part of the problem. We are taught that good parents do whatever it takes to rid their children of "bad" behavior. When the behavior isn't corrected with technique number one, a parent puts more time, effort, and attention into finding another technique. Negative, bad, pesky, problematic, or challenging behaviors equal weeds. Ineffective parenting strategies equal the fertilizer. It's as simple as that.

At this point, it's reasonable for a parent to wonder how exactly those pesky behaviors get started in the first place. First, though, it's important for parents to understand that the pesky behaviors begin merely by accident.

Planting Weeds

Do you remember when you brought your first child home? Do you remember wanting to keep your baby close to you so you could gaze into those eyes and keep a steady maternal connection, even though you really needed to get up and take a shower? Do you remember finally putting your sweet bundle down so you could dash to the bathroom for a much-needed shower, only to find yourself sticking your head out a dozen times to listen to the baby monitor, just in case the baby should wake up and need you? When your infant made his first fussing noises, you probably did what most first-time parents do: you sprinted to the room, scooped the cherub up, and began cooing to reassure your baby that you were indeed paying attention to him!

It's easy to see in this context how we rush in and pay attention when our children are babies, by shushing, lulling, and appeasing them, so they stay happy, quiet, and content. Don't get me wrong: this makes perfect sense, since our babies can

Duct Tape Moment

Tape those toes to the ground and give your baby the chance to experiment with what happens when she coos and cries. It isn't a bad thing to let her see what type of communication she can develop with you. If you come running at every whimper, she'll have you trained! Duct tape your feet to the ground and turn your sprint to a stroll.

only communicate through one set of sounds. However, something bigger begins with this tendency.

Kids, from birth, are in the process of doing two things simultaneously:

1. Unconsciously developing behaviors that will guarantee their primary caregivers attend to them in a quick and timely fashion until they are independent enough to tend to themselves. The kids are in the process of training their parents, not the other way around.

2. Establishing their place or role within the family. During this infancy phase, parents unintentionally assist in the development or deconstruction of behaviors, depending on the focus and energy they give each behavior the child exhibits. Whatever behavior gets the most attention continues to grow; the behaviors that are ignored fade away. The role the child develops over time within the family structure, good or bad, will ultimately determine how he views himself in connection to a larger world. In other words, it will become the child's self-ideal.

Understanding what's happening for your children might make it easier for you to look at a particular behavior as something other than just annoying, irritating, or bad. If you can understand the motivation for a behavior, the emotional charge you feel is likely to decrease and a new kind of clarity and calm will develop during your interactions with your child.

Who Is Really Doing the Training?

Let's continue with the rush to "soothe" a fussing baby. Initially, children do whatever they can to gain the attention of their parents, and they do this as a survival tactic. Obviously, at this level, they are completely dependent upon others, and if they cannot find ways to bring their parents to them and care for their needs, they will not survive. This is strong motivation for children to develop a behavior pattern that has mom and dad running to their side. I know it sounds primal. It is.

Because of this helplessness, which we are programmed to protect, parents spend time rushing to the newborn's mews, no matter the reason for the crying. Without the parents realizing it, however, the baby quickly trains the parents to react, providing special attention even when it's not a matter of basic needs. Eventually, parents notice that whenever they even think of putting the baby down the child begins to fuss. It's as if the baby *knows* mommy is getting ready to put her down. Here's where parents commit to the idea of making the fussiness go away and sign up to give more attention to this behavior than is necessary.

This first weed (unnecessary fussiness) isn't exactly pleasant, and it has itty-bitty roots, but it can quickly grow into a habit. If mom jumps each time her infant begins to fuss, she will often continue jumping when her toddler and preschooler fuss (which now sounds like whining). It's not unusual for a parent who begins to feel trapped in this dynamic to manufacture "stories" that justify her decision to carry a two-year-old around as if he were still an infant.

Is the point I am making that you shouldn't carry your baby around when she cries? Of course not. You can, and many parents do, but it's very important that parents notice what their behavior is doing to nourish a potential weed. Eventually, for every parent, the decision to swoop in and react will set off the photosynthesis cycle and the sprouts will start to bud. Parents must pay attention to their role in the relationship right from the beginning. Carrying the child wasn't a big deal until he turned into a three-year-old who wouldn't leave mom's side, slept in the bed with mom and dad, and refused to engage with anyone other than mom. Of course, this wasn't mom's intention when she started jumping at the first sign of fussing, but that is how easy it is for a once small weed to shoot upward and take over. The effects begin to spill into the real world: getting out the door becomes exceptionally difficult, leaving for a dinner date is a nightmare, and various other outings where mother and child must separate are far more exhausting than is necessary or healthy.

Remember, when kids are very young, they aren't able to understand anything we say, but they do understand our body language, our actions, our tone, and our attitude. If the goal for the child is to draw mom and dad closer, then whatever it takes to accomplish that goal is logical to the child. The bigger the reaction kids receive from their parents, the more likely they are to continue using the behavior. It isn't malicious, it isn't calculating, and it isn't meant to drive you crazy. It's as simple as cause and effect.

Weeds Become Labels
That Define Our Kids

While kids are learning effective ways to engage mom and dad and thereby assure their continued survival, something else is happening that further impacts the weed/fertilizer cycle. Children are also in the process of developing a sense of how they fit in or belong within the family structure, and they do this by internalizing parental responses to any and all of their behavior. Unfortunately, most parents aren't aware that their child is evolving into the whiner, the crier, the tattler, the noodler, or the baby talker, as a result of their swift and dedicated responses and efforts to make the behavior stop. Once a child is accustomed to consistent, clear communication every time she does X, Y, or Z, the root of the weed takes hold and will continue to grow as the cycle continues. By now, the metaphor is clear. You get more of what you don't want (weeds) by paying attention to (fertilizing) them.

What might still be a bit hazy is the answer to this question: Why would my smart, adorable kid keep acting this way if his behavior only precipitates anger and frustration on my part and leads to some sort of punishment or discord? The answer is this: your child is answering one question over and over again, "In my family I am the child who…?" A parent's consistent. engaged, and emotional response to the behavior confirms for the child their place within the family and so it continues, sometimes for days, sometimes for years. When asked, parents generally agree that a child's negative behavior provokes emotionally charged, consistent responses from them while positive behavior from a child evokes calm, unemotional, even responses. In a child's mind, the intensity and consistency of the response is what counts. Now, I am not suggesting that you go over the top and start commenting on every positive behavior your child exhibits. This is an equally slippery slope into ineffective parenting and we will cover that in section 2. Right now, I am making the point that the tendency of parents is to focus on what they don't want, and that is why these weeds grow wild in our homes.

Tales from Weedville

Have you ever heard a parent say to a child, "As soon as you use a big girl voice, I will get you some juice"? We know the mom is thinking, *"If I keep pointing out how much I want the whining to stop, eventually it will."*

What we don't realize is that the child is thinking, *I can get my mom to look at me and talk to me just by using a whiney voice. This is how I keep mom engaged with me and this is who I am in the family.*

Sure enough, the next time the little girl wants something, she makes her plea with a high-pitched, nasally, "Mommyyyy, can I have some chocolate miiiilk?" And that's how it goes, back and forth, until the mother, who can't stand the whining, is forced to verbally label her own child a whiner, because it's all she can see and hear and focus on. She couldn't make the whining stop, no matter how hard she tried, so she accepted her child as the incarnate whiner. Dutifully, the child fulfilled her mother's expectation.

Here's a true story that illustrates one family's experience as it discovered how big a weed could grow.

Whining Works Just Fine for Emily

Emily, at age five, loved to whine. She had played out her toddler and preschool years as the whiner in the family. Emily's mother, Jan, had been dealing with this situation the same way for four years without getting the results she wanted. Her strategies for tackling this weed included telling her child:

> "Emily, I cannot talk to you when you use your whiney voice."
> "Emily, I am counting—one...two...three..."
> "Emily, you will have to go to time-out if you don't stop whining."
> "Emily, use your big girl voice and then I will talk to you."
> "Emily, people will not talk to you if you continue to use your whiney voice."
> "Emily, I will answer you when you use your other voice."

Then, as kindergarten approached for Emily, she and her mother had several conversations about the appropriate voice a child should use in school and with her teacher. Mom explained to Emily that she might be teased at school or that people would assume that she wasn't as smart as she actually

Duct Tape Moment

Simply seal your mouth and stop verbally fertilizing the whiney "weed." And yes, if you're saying to your child, "I can't talk to you while you're whining," guess what? You're still talking! Hold your tongue and your reactions until your wee one stumbles onto another voice and then—make the connection.

was because she used the whiney voice. In honesty, mom was trying everything she possibly could to ensure that Emily entered kindergarten with a mature and likeable personality. There's nothing wrong with Jan's intention, but her approach was putting her through the emotional wringer!

On the first day of school, Emily walked into the classroom and said in her whiniest voice, "Mrs. Morgan, my mom told me that I should talk to you about sitting in the front row, because I get wiggly and need to pay extra attention." Mrs. Morgan looked down at Emily and said, "Emily you are in kindergarten, and from now on I want you to use your 'big girl voice' each day when you arrive to school. Do you understand me?" With a big smile, Emily responded, "Oh yes, Mrs. Morgan. I understand completely."

Here was another adult in Emily's life who would focus on the very thing her mother had been focusing on each and every day of Emily's young life. What do you think came up at parent meetings? And notes home? Exactly. It wasn't until Emily went to first grade that things changed. We'll get to the story of Emily's change in chapter 7.

Now that you have a clearer understanding of this cycle, here are a few more stories to illustrate what weeds look like in real families.

I Found Something to Do to Drive Mom Bonkers

Jada has two sons. They generally get along, but during certain stretches of the day, the boys can be counted on to tease each other until it escalates into a full-fledged fight.

Jack, eight years old, WHAPS James, six.

James screams, "He hit me!"

Mom runs in and says, "Stop it right now and both of you find something else to do." She walks out.

Duct Tape Moment

Glue that gluteus maximus into a far-away chair—outside, in the other room, or at the neighbor's house if you have to! Do not get up and go running in to referee. The exchange will end faster without a megaphone and a spotlight. Plus, it proves you have something better to do than get involved with nonsense.

James teases Jack for several minutes until Jack SMACKS James.

James screeches, "MOM! He hit me again!"

Mom returns and, as if caught in a revolving door, she revisits the scene a handful of times until she's so irritated that she shuts off the television and demands the two boys separate, adding a nice lecture for good measure.

Mom looks at Jack and says, "Stop picking on your brother! You're being a bully." She turns her attention to James and asks, "Are you hurt?"

The next day, a similar scene unfolds, and Jada starts in with, "Why can't you be nice to each other?" She adds, "I'm taking your screen time away until the two of you can treat each other with some respect."

And so it goes, day after day, week after week, until an attention-seeking, aggressive weed is growing healthy and full in the living room. The boys have grown to expect their mother's attention and strong reaction to their fighting. Jada's younger son is never hurt badly during these skirmishes and, despite being slightly annoyed, he also feeds into them by teasing his brother and then telling on him. Her older son is gaining a reputation for being antagonistic toward others and will eventually be labeled a bully, but he takes no real pleasure in hurting his brother.

Over time, mom's laser focus on her son's disturbing behavior and the labels she has assigned them actually feed the sport. Mom is holding the watering can, ready to add some more tender care with every single correction, punishment, lecture, and so forth. Does this mean that a parent never addresses the problem of fighting between siblings? Absolutely not. The point here is to realize that what you are doing now is making it worse.

There's a Weed Growing in My Bed

As an infant, Angela slept with mom and dad in their bed. At the time, it seemed like the sensible thing to do, as Evelyn was nursing and the arrangement provided them all with much-needed sleep. Evelyn and Tony planned on putting their daughter into a crib in her own room by the time she was three or four months old, but each time they tried to move their infant, she fussed, cried, woke up, and, ultimately, ended up back in bed with her mom and dad. They tried a number of creative tactics to deal with the sleeping issue, but were met with defeat at each new attempt. Angela had more determination, tenacity, and staying power than her parents and she won the battle of the sleeping arrangements.

Fast-forward five years, and Angela is either coming into her parents' room for a final snuggle or mom and dad are spending forty-five minutes sitting with her as she falls asleep. No one in the family is getting the rest they require, Angela is tired for kindergarten, and the sleeping arrangement is putting undue stress on Evelyn and Tony's relationship. Inadvertently, mom and dad are feeding the "unnecessary attachment" weed, which is eroding the confidence of their child and causing tension between the couple. They thought, as many parents do, that talking with Angela about the sleeping arrangements, using different techniques to deal with the issue, threatening, and then bribing Angela in order to get her to put herself to sleep would eventually result in a daughter capable of letting go and falling asleep on her own but all the attention and focus only compounded the problem.

Seven-Year-Old Genius Shoplifter in Aisle Eight

Stealing candy is a bad thing, right? Yes, it's illegal and wrong by moral standards. However, sweet-faced Lily, all of seven years old, has found a very clear and consistent way to get her mother to drop everything and share some quality, emotionally invested time with her. This behavior first appeared when Lily was only three and she took her brother's favorite truck from his room to her room. Mom seized the opportunity to lecture Lily about not taking what wasn't hers and, from that moment, a small weed took hold. Over the years, Lily continued to take what wasn't hers until her mom landed on the idea

Duct Tape Moment

Zip the lips and stay calm and do not let your fears of what might happen drive you to hyperfocus on "making it stop." The more you treat the child like a thief and talk about her behavior as bad, the more she'll show up and play the role of thief. Choose another trait to focus on, and soon the "clepto" tendencies will fade away and the real Lily will make her appearance.

that Lily was "stealing." Once the label was established, mom went about trying to get Lily to stop.

Now, at seven, all Lily has to do is grab a lip gloss on the way out of the department store, stash a book from the library in her backpack, or swipe candy from the checkout, and her mother's overreaction occurs like clockwork. To deal with this pesky weed of "stealing," mom will meet with teachers, enlist the help of Lily's grandparents to talk with Lily, lecture, punish, and finally try bribing Lily as a way to make the stealing stop.

With an endless supply of attention focused on the very behavior mom is trying to extinguish, the weed grabs hold and grows unchecked. Lily can not only guarantee attention from mom, but also from the checkout people, the librarian, and anyone who either witnesses her sleight of hand or is subject to one of her many apologies. In any case, she sits through lectures or looks of disapproval. Mom understands that if she doesn't nip this in the bud, it could be a real problem in years to come, and she is genuinely concerned. Mom is committed to quashing her daughter's behavior, and so the weed buds again.

Look over Here Everybody, I'm Noodling

Blaine was born into a fast-paced, get-up-and-go family. Unfortunately Blaine wasn't a get-up-and-go kind of kid. He did things his own way, in his own time, and it was clear from the beginning, by his relaxed nursing style, that he was not interested in rushing through the day. Before Blaine could even walk, Kathy and her husband, Bryan, had already started to focus on the fact that Blaine was easily distracted and slowed the whole family down. They used a number of tactics to keep Blaine moving, but if they ceased their prodding, Blaine would disengage within minutes, wander away, and the cycle would begin again.

Duct Tape Moment

Cover your mouth to prevent yourself from coaxing and commenting on the child's role in the family routine. Instead, focus on pace of the routine and remember that your child's actions are his choice but your reaction is your choice. Let him go slowly but pay no attention to it—he will not find it so amusing once you've moved on. The trick here is to not get emotionally engaged in his shenanigans. Make a mask out of the tape if you have to! Focus your attention on the routine and encourage his budding independence.

This continued into the preschool years and on into elementary school. When his parents were trying to leave, Blaine was off playing. When it was time for dinner, he was playing on the computer. When it was time to do homework, he was getting supplies, setting up the space, and getting one more glass of water. Blaine noodled his way through life, and, from his perspective, there was no reason to change his behavior in any way. Mom and dad, though, were sick of nudging and reminding and then bribing and eventually resorting to empty threats to keep him on task.

"We're leaving without you!"

"If you run out of time, the science project stays on the table."

"If you don't get your ski boots on, we're skiing without you and you can sit in the lodge with a babysitter."

On the threats went, with no progress being made in speeding up the child's pace. Blaine was no faster or more willing to pay attention and get things done when he was a toddler.

Kids figure out which behaviors trigger big, consistent

responses from parents and which do not. If it is a child's desire to engage with a parent, Blaine clearly won this game.

Sit Down. Charlie, Come Back. Sit.

Charlie, at nine years old, is still struggling to sit at the table and enjoy a meal with his parents. When Charlie was very young, he squirmed whenever anyone but mom tried to feed him. He wouldn't sit in his highchair without screaming, and so Amy took to feeding him on her lap. Before long, Charlie was being fed in mom's lap off of mom's plate. Any attempt to put Charlie in a chair to eat turned into a large-scale temper tantrum that ended with Charlie back on his mom's lap. Each meal began the same way, with a quick lecture to Charlie about staying in his chair to eat like a big boy. Sometimes Amy and Joe added a bribe at the end of the lecture if Charlie stayed in his chair or a punishment if he moved from his chair.

This story, like the others, illustrates that the simple dynamic of cause and effect plays a powerful role in the weed/fertilizer cycle. In this case Charlie had it figured out long

Duct Tape Moment

Put a piece of tape over your mouth and wrists, securing yourself to the dining chair. You don't move, lecture, bribe, punish, nag, or play along. Let the little guy do his thing—it's his choice to mess around. It's your choice to react differently. Just sit and wait. Once he gets up from the table, untether yourself, remove his plate, and it's over. No emotion—he'll be fine. In fact, he'll be better next time because if he's hungry, he'll eat.

before his parents did; he knew that he controlled dinner, and mom and dad would do anything to get him to act like a big boy who sat at the table. Now, at nine, the family is stuck in a game of round-and-round that leaves all of them feeling frustrated and defeated. What would happen if Charlie no longer had an audience? What if mom and dad stopped feeding the weed?

EXERCISE: IDENTIFY THE WEEDS

Take a moment to list all the pesky behaviors your children engage in that, if they stopped, would make all your lives more enjoyable. Use the sentence below to get yourself thinking and consult the chart for ideas. Put a star next to the big, beefy ones.

Fill in the blanks in this sentence:

If my child just stopped _____ (insert weed), _____ (daytime, bedtime, dinner) life would be so much _____ (easier, happier, mellower, more relaxing, enjoyable.)

Don't worry. You won't be judged. It's important that you are honest, so that your list will help you and the weed will become a thing of the past.

Useless, Pesky, Naughty, Bad, Disrespectful Behavior

Fighting	Getting up from the table	Arguing
Hitting		Making a mess
Biting	Getting out of bed	Losing things
Whining	Disrespecting your stuff	Forgetting homework
Throwing things		
Ignoring you	Mouthing off	Intimidating people
Teasing	Talking back	Engaging in power struggles
Throwing tantrums	Refusing to eat	
	Being unwilling to pick up stuff	

EXERCISE: IDENTIFY YOUR RESPONSE

Now that you have your list of weeds, finish the formula by identifying how you feel and the way you react to the weed.

Each weed elicits a certain feeling or emotion in you, making you annoyed, frustrated, hurt, embarrassed, disappointed, or angry, and causes a reaction, such as nagging, reminding, lecturing, counting, scolding, yelling, and so on. One thing is for sure, both the feeling and the reaction are likely strong, consistent, and emotionally charged.

Make a list of the ways you feel about the behavior and all the ways you react when you spot the weed.

Fill in the blanks in this sentence:

Whenever I hear/see _____ (child) do this _____ (weed), I feel _____ (emotion) and immediately _____ (reaction).

Write it out fifty times if you have fifty weeds. Be honest and admit, *Hey, I don't like yelling or bribing or melting down.* This is for you. You're going to see change, so lay it all out here.

Here's a list to get you thinking:

Your Emotions/Feelings		Your Response	
Angry	Depressed	Nagging	Judging
Embarrassed	Incompetent	Reminding	Belittling
Disrespected	Defeated	Lecturing	Making fun of
Weak	Protective	Yelling	Theorizing
Powerless	Ignored	Threatening	Demanding
Frustrated	Overwhelmed	Punishing	Throwing things
Hopeless	Disregarded	Bribing	Slamming doors
Infuriated	Out of control	Saving	Walking away upset

Your Emotions/Feelings		Your Response	
Morally affected	Stressed out	Taking things away	Interjecting
Physically concerned	Exhausted	Counting	Correcting
Impatient	Failed	Giving time-outs	Pretending it's okay
Defensive	Annoyed	Moralizing	just this time
Irritated	Tired	Doing for	Exiling
Compelled to stop	Confused	Using sarcasm	Coddling
Worried	Ashamed	Guilt-tripping	Refusing
Afraid	Disgraced	Shaming	Defending
Rushed	Incapable	Ostracizing	Making excuses
Disorganized	Misunderstood	Ridiculing (unintention-	Giving up (until
Insulted	Sad	ally or	next time)
Disgusted	Miserable	intentionally)	Power tripping
Flabbergasted	Oppressed	Interfering	
	Bothered		

More Thoughts on Weeds

Like weeds, pesky, useless behaviors grow back over and over again unless you get to the root! You may have heard, "Don't worry about it. It's just a phase. He will grow out of it in time." Unfortunately, this couldn't be further from the truth.

If you are thinking, like most parents I work with, that your children will suddenly grow out of a particularly pesky behavior because it was just a phase; it's time to flip that thought. Children don't grow *out of*, they grow *into*, whatever they are currently doing. This includes both positive and negative behaviors. Your children will never, no matter how hard you wish, hit a magical age and suddenly walk down the stairs one morning and declare that they have seen the light and the errors of their ways. They will not magically say to you, "Mom l Dad, I am so sorry for my disrespectful attitude. I totally understand why I should pick up my stuff instead of dumping it on the floor for you to pick up." Obviously, that's not realistic. Neither is the assumption that behaviors are childish and will go away. Some very childish behaviors are being used for far bigger reasons than childish entertainment. The big, beefy, problematic behaviors, the ones that drive us the craziest, are the ones that most often stick around for years and years.

Children become more determined and anchored in behavior the longer they use it. And again, the more you try to get your child to give up the problematic behavior, the more anchored it becomes.

If you have any doubt about whether your kids' behaviors will stick around, think about the adults you know who:

- Are habitually late
- Whine
- Are bossy
- Are overwhelmed
- Are tattletales
- Are disorganized
- Fight with others
- Blame others
- Don't deal with frustration or stress in healthy ways
- Are manipulative
- Are compulsive
- And so forth

Do not underestimate the power these weeds can have over the course of a lifetime. They influence personality, habits, and, most of all, confidence. Pesky behaviors, weeds, don't make people unlovable or unaccepted or unsuccessful as adults, but they do present an unflattering side to an otherwise wonderful human being and can fracture a family dynamic. I'd say that we all have a few weeds we wish we'd pulled long ago.

Weeds: A Quick Overview

Weeds are the pesky behaviors that can quickly dominate and define the relationship you have with your children. The weeds grow bigger and stronger the more you try to get rid of them. This attention is the fertilizer that keeps the weed growing.

Between the ages of birth and five years, children experiment with a variety of behaviors designed to answer two questions: (1) How do I ensure that I can engage my caregivers quickly and consistently to ensure my survival? and (2) How do I define myself? In other words, what is my role within the family? The behaviors that garner the biggest reaction are anchored and can grow over the course of a lifetime as your child anchors his identity with a weed or weeds (the victim, the whiner, the blamer, and so on). By consistently focusing and paying attention to behaviors, you reinforce these behaviors, making them part of the daily interactions that define the child and your relationship. Children continue to use the behaviors more often and with more tenacity. You can't seem to get them to stop.

If you have a child older than three years old, you know that she is growing *into* this behavior not out of it. Teachers, coaches, grandparents, babysitters, and others may react the same way, keeping the habit afloat. If the cycle is not broken and children do not have the opportunity to redefine themselves and develop more useful behavior, it can lead to major problems in confidence and the ability to navigate the real world.

It's Up to You to Turn off the Sprinkler

Sometimes it helps to look at the situation this way: your children are brilliant, because from their perspective nothing is wrong. They are getting what they want. They have you trained, and in certain situations, they are in control of the way the family functions. You can be relied upon to do the same thing over and over again even though you experience little or no long-term change. Your kids are merely doing what they have always done, and for them, it is working perfectly.

Change what you do, and your children's behavior will change. That's where we're going here. What exactly can you do to dry up the weeds? I'll give you a hint: put them in a dark closet and they will quietly disappear within a few short weeks.

Duct Tape Moment

Grab a box, gather the weeds you don't want in your life, and place them inside this box. Next, tape it up so tightly that no air, light, or love can get inside. Don't open the box, shake the box, or peek inside it to give the weeds another round of attention. And don't bring the box out in public or at family events or in teacher conferences. Once it's away, it's not a subject for conversation. (Think of how quickly we forget what we have stored in the back of our closets—put this box up there with the old popcorn maker and candlesticks you got for your wedding. You don't need to have them hanging around, taking up valuable space.)

2

Band-Aids on Bullet Wounds: Your Strategy Is the Problem

You need to fix what's broken first, before you put
something else on top of it.

—*Bonnie Taylor*

When it comes to parenting, there are only two
problems, lack of training or a fractured relationship,
both of which are worth fixing.

—*Vicki Hoefle*

In chapter 1, we exposed the cornucopia of strategies, techniques, and tools employed by parents to deal with the bad,
annoying, irresponsible, undesirable, and otherwise pesky
behaviors their children present, and the list is extensive. Not
only do these ineffective and confusing strategies become
the focus (the fertilizer) that anchors the negative behaviors
(the weeds), they are also responsible for making things worse
because they are used so haphazardly.

It's hard work for moms and dads to stay on top of all the
scripts, carrots, action–reaction rehearsals, and do-this-not-
that advice they've picked up from the web, television, books,
friends, and their own parents. It's also hard for them to figure out when to use them, how to use them, and how often

to use them. This confusion leads to what I call the "Band-Aid" approach to parenting. The kids are yelling, so you use a Band-Aid tactic to get them to stop, so you can get to the car on time. The yelling might stop for a minute, but before long it pops its head back up, and then it's back to the box of Band-Aids again. I find the Band-Aid tactics parents employ fall into two categories.

1. Recognized parenting strategies
   - Time-outs
   - Naughty chair
   - Lecturing
   - Sending to room
   - Taking away screen time
   - Grounding
   - Punishing
   - Taking away privileges
   - Bribing
   - Counting

These Band-Aid tactics might be easily recognizable, popular, and accepted, but they do little to create long-term change and do a great deal to fracture relationships.

2. Default parenting strategies
   - Yelling: "Get your shoes on! Let's go! Let's go!"
   - Convincing: "Hey, you should really bring an umbrella. Yes, it's going to rain, you don't want to get wet."
   - Talking through: "Okay, guys, when we get there, how should we behave?" Play by play, "Say thank you, now do this, now do that."
   - Saving: "Well, okay, this time I'll bring your homework to you."

- Reminding: "Remember your uniform. Don't forget your cleats." (Day after day after day.)
- Intervening: "You two stop that." Repeat.
- Threatening: "If you don't stop, I will send you to your room when we get home."

These tactics are used in a haphazard way when parents feel they must do something to deal with a behavior or rectify a situation. There doesn't seem to be any rhyme or reason to their use, and they almost always make things worse.

Whether a parent uses a recognized or a default Band-Aid tactic the results are the same. The tactics amplify power struggles, leave parents and children feeling confused and defeated, fracture their relationship further, and rarely bring any lasting or substantial change to the situation or to the behavior the parent is trying to eliminate.

This reality was one of the driving forces behind my finding a better way than Band-Aiding the behavior problems that presented themselves throughout the day. If I wanted my kids to get to bed on time, without a thirty-minute meltdown that led to screaming and tears, it didn't make sense for me to "fix" the routine with one-hit-wonder tactics that might prove gold for a moment but would fade into a blur by the next evening. The same thing went for getting out of the door in the morning or dining out as a family. I wasn't organized enough to use a time-out at home (five different ways with five kids) and a bribery trick at dinner and "just one more story tonight" to keep things running smoothly at bedtime.

Peel-and-stick Band-Aid tactics are used to "stop the bleeding" of the moment and get life moving, but they do not deliver long-term, sustainable change, and they don't establish order, harmony, respect, or cooperation between family members. The bottom line is that if a strategy doesn't deliver lasting change and make the job of parenting fun and exciting, I'm not doing it. What would your life be like if parenting was fun and exciting and life with your kids was full of peace, harmony, cooperation, and respect?

Here's the story of Mary, a mother I worked with who went through this cycle. Maybe you can identify with her.

Just for Today? Yeah, Right!

On Monday morning, after a particularly enjoyable weekend during which all the kids got along and their actions suggested that everyone in the family was in a really good place, Mary had high hopes that she and the kids would make it through their morning, into the car, and off to school with no problems. Mary was certain that they could all continue riding the high they were feeling and leverage it into a scream-free morning.

But when Mary heard the first nasally whine come from her four-year-old, followed by an exasperated "Shut up" from her six-year-old, followed by a contemptuous "Who used the toilet without flushing?" from her nine-year-old, she knew the honeymoon was over. That good weekend could've come down to luck, weather patterns, and a good night's sleep. Who knows what it was, but it didn't, as Mary had daydreamed, carry over to Monday.

Like many parents, Mary let her wishful thinking and reliance on Band-Aid tactics (instead of an intentional parenting plan) lead the way. She woke up to face the day with a belief in miracles and a deep sense of hope that things would be different, and when they weren't, she was right back to, "Knock it off! Be nice, don't say shut up. Seriously? Someone go flush. Do you have your stuff? Did you brush your teeth? Stop fighting!" and on and on until she swung through the minivan

Duct Tape Moment

Tape your tush to the chair, secure a cup of coffee in your hand, toss two pieces of tape over your ears, and stick one over your mouth. Sit, sip (lift the tape to sip!), and do not exercise the urge to jump in and fan the wildfire! These kids know they ought to flush and brush their teeth but the song and dance is part of the routine—you don't need to listen to it or participate in playing along, and they can do it without all the jumping in and flipping out! So, pretend you don't even hear it and take the "quiet time" to make a plan that will work in the long term.

drop-off line, shooing her children out as they continued to squabble.

Once the kids were gone and the car was quiet, Mary let out a huge sigh, but within the hour she began to dread the pickup and the afternoon she would spend in the same trap. That fresh start she dreamed about earlier that morning was now a streaked, stained mess.

Even though, deep down, Mary didn't really believe life would be different after one relaxing weekend, she went for the wish and inadvertently signed herself up for another day parenting from a "quick fix" mentality. Let's face it, if she had to wager, she'd have bet on the morning breaking down, but she gambled with her morning instead. She'd agreed to the "I'll deal with it when it happens" approach.

But this Band-Aid story doesn't stop here. Like so many parents, Mary went to bed feeling lousy about her day as a parent, frustrated with the kids for being such jerks (her word), and promising herself, *Tomorrow it's going to be different*. Without a solid plan in place, Mary hits the desperation mode, and desperation mode brings out even more Band-Aid tactics.

The next morning, Mary sounded like this:

"Tommy, I will help you get dressed today, but tomorrow you have to do this on your own. I know you know how to get dressed by yourself."

"Adam, I'm going to help you get your homework organized and into your backpack today, but tomorrow you're going to have to take care of this all by yourself. I know you know how to do this and it's time for you to start getting organized by yourself in the morning."

"Emma, I will make you some toast with peanut butter this morning, because I know you're running late, but from now on you will have to take care of this yourself in the morning."

Mary made these same kinds of parenting decisions, better described as concessions, with her kids throughout the day: "I'll carry your coat today, but tomorrow you'll have to be a big boy and carry it yourself."

"Adam, I'll bring you your soccer shoes to practice today, but this is the last time I'm going to do this."

"Emma, I will run to the store to get you what you need for your project, but from now on you are going to have to be more organized."

This continued on all day long.

Mary knew that she switched her tactics from harsh and demanding on Monday to maid service on Tuesday, and that on Wednesday, she would probably pull out a completely different set of Band-Aid tactics. The most frustrating part of this cycle for Mary was that she knew her kids were capable of so much more and that in spite of this knowledge, she had no idea what to do to change things.

Mary was caught in a trap, and she had no idea how to get out of it. In the back of her mind she knew she was raising her children with more strain, stress, frustration, and anxiety than was necessary or enjoyable for anybody! When the dictating and prompting and reminding did not work, she bribed the kids to do what she wanted in the moment or, depending upon her mood, she might just give in and do it for them. As she tired of that strategy or found she hadn't slept well the night before, it was just as likely that she would threaten them into doing what she wanted. The only thing consistent with her parenting was that she would work very hard to make tomorrow better because today, frankly, stunk. Not only was she jumping from one Band-Aid tactic to another, she was also feeding the weed with all her focus on the negative.

Here's where I jumped in with a little commentary. I explained to Mary that she was making the majority of her parenting decisions based on external forces and flip-flopping quick fixes depending on her own mood and stress level. She cared more about getting things done and being prepared and on time than she did about training the kids on how to take care of their own morning routines. She cared more about the hairy eyeball she got from the grocery clerk than she did about teaching her kids how to actually help her at the grocery store. She cared more about the "tsk-tsks" she received from teachers and coaches when her kids came to school or their sporting events unprepared than she did about taking the time to teach her kids how to prepare for their own lives.

When I suggested to Mary that her reactions could be compared to putting a Band-Aid on a bullet wound, I saw the "aha" in her eyes, and she smiled for the first time in the forty-five minutes she'd been explaining her dilemma to me.

Mary admitted, "That is exactly what it feels like to me. I can see myself opening the Band-Aid box, reaching in, getting a small Band-Aid for a big problem, and thinking to myself, *Oh, what difference does it make if I do it today? I'll get serious about solving the problem tomorrow.* I put the Band-Aid on the bullet wound, just like you said, and four hours later it's gushing blood all over again. This visual is going to help me hold myself accountable when I am tempted to go for the quick fix."

This visual may be helpful to you as well. In order to break the habit of sticking Band-Aids on bullet wounds, you first have to be clear about what the bullet wounds are. After twenty years as a parent educator, I can tell you that, just as there are two categories of Band-Aid tactics, recognized and default, most challenges in the home fall into two distinct categories: lack of training and fractured relationship challenges (otherwise known as bullet wounds).

Training Bullet Wound

With this type of bullet wound, the kids aren't trained to take care of all the things they could be handling in their daily lives, which means that you are micromanaging, nagging, reminding, saving, bribing, and so on, just to get through the day. Until the kids are trained and are cooperating on a regular basis within the family, you will continue to use Band-Aid tactics just to get through the day.

For Mary, many of the daily challenges with the kids could have been avoided had she taken the time to train the kids to take on more responsibility in their lives. Instead, she did things for the kids that they could have done for themselves. Like many parents, she believed that by doing things for her kids, she could avoid power struggles, make life easier for everyone, and limit conflicts. Unfortunately, the opposite occurred. Because the kids weren't trained and no systems were in place, Mary was forced to micromanage, nag, remind, punish, bribe, and save just to get through the day.

Most parents get into this untrained-kid, reaction-strategy cycle without noticing at first, because it's tolerable and the day eventually (usually) balances out. Parents often are willing to trade a moment of chaos for a moment of quiet. It's not fun or ideal, but it doesn't leave them feeling like total failures. However, over time parents become exhausted and resentful. As the ebb and flow starts to crash and tip, it becomes obvious that the fixes are not working and the parents are working way too hard implementing Band-Aid tactics that just don't work.

Repairing the training bullet wound takes patience and creativity, consistency, and yes, more patience. It's linear, built on a system that grows over time. At first, the kids learn how to fold their own laundry, then put it away, then wash it, then dry it, and so forth, until you don't have the sock meltdown because your eight-year-old is doing his own laundry and knows exactly where his socks are. Suddenly, you don't need a Band-Aid for that.

What else? Well, the kids won't have time to mess around and squabble with each other if they're making lunches or feeding the fish or packing their sports bags or calling the teacher to find out about extra credit. It's a system that steers parents and kids away from the back-and-forth to a more solid, united style of moving forward together as a family.

When the kids know how to manage their lives and are doing so on a regular basis, the game changes. Not only is the house running smoothly and mom can take time to enjoy life, but the kids develop confidence, because they are participating in and making decisions about their own lives.

As we saw with Mary, the kids were disconnected from their lives. Mary was in charge of everything, including maintaining the schedule, managing the fights, remembering belongings, and keeping everyone happy. The kids couldn't have cared less. They weren't feeling downtrodden or belittled as they hopped out of the minivan, they were merely on to the next part of the day's schedule; mom took care of it all and the kids created mischief.

Relationship Bullet Wound

Relationship wounds are more serious and manifest themselves as power struggles, bullying, fighting, talking back, sassing, lying, insulting, defying, blaming, and other negative interactions between parents and their children. Parents reserve the bigger, sturdier Band-Aids for this type of bullet wound, and because of the emotional intensity, parents are led to greater feelings of failure and frustration when the strategies they are using do not produce change.

If the relationship between you and your kids is fractured in some way, it's probably reflected in one or all of these dynamics. We see power struggles, breakdowns in communication, snarky attitudes, fights, disrespect, disconnection, and cruelty all dealt with by punishing, lecturing, moralizing, bribing, reminding, and so on. Until the entire family learns to invest in healthy, respectful relationships, Mary will continue to use Band-Aid tactics to dole out punishment for "bad" behavior, use control to avoid explosive episodes, and threaten in order to get the kids to behave.

Parents who do resort to quick-fix strategies to cover, rather than repair, an injured relationship will soon find they are emotionally and mentally exhausted. Generally, parents in this cycle know it right away and they feel a much more critical need to make things better, or put out the fire, because everyone can end up miserable within minutes.

Over time, as parents, we notice these relationship-bullet-wound behaviors resurface over and over in the child's life (remember how we said they don't grow *out of* a behavior, they grow *into* it). For example, an angry toddler is an angry tween is an angry teen. Some of it can be attributed to personality, but once a cycle of behavior emerges without any resolution, parents often adopt feelings of hopelessness and anger and a strong desire to throw their hands in the air. Parents feel like giving up, because they haven't been able to repair the fragile relationship with their child. A parent will never be able to use a time-out to remove the anger from a child; they could, however, learn to repair the relationship and watch the anger lift.

If you are experiencing this type of emotional turmoil when you force a Band-Aid on a problem, and if you are ready for a change, you must be willing to accept the problem for what it really is, an injury to the relationship. If you understand that the relationship has been injured, that Band-Aid tactics will only make it worse, and you are open to doing something different, you are on your way to enjoying your children and throwing your box of Band-Aids into the nearest garbage can.

This new thinking will help you make the shift into a more sustainable parenting practice. I know firsthand that parents raising kids in the twenty-first century are faced with enormous pressures, technological influences, and a whole new frontier of challenges never before navigated. The time and energy required to create intentional, thoughtful parenting strategies is more and more difficult for parents. It's easy to find yourself in a cycle of quick-fix solutions without really comprehending what the long-term effects might be for you and your kids. I understand it's easier to say, *I will train them tomorrow because it's too inconvenient right now. I don't have the time.* I also understand that if parents want to achieve smoother days, calmer nights, and more enjoyable time together in between, they have to commit to new thinking (which you're learning here) and new approaches (which we'll get to in the chapters ahead).

This chart illustrates what Band-Aids look like and why parents are even bothering to use them. In the solutions section of this book, we'll talk more about what you can do that will help with training and what you can do to repair and deepen the relationship with your children. For our purposes here, we are just going to point out what parents do and why they go for the short-term, quick-fix, Band-Aid tactic. This awareness will help with understanding and implementation later on in the book.

Band-Aid	Why Parents Use It
Reminding: *"Tell your aunt thank you for the wonderful gift, Gail."*	So kids don't look rude and embarrass *me*.
Bribing: *"If you are the first to the car today, you can sit in whatever seat you want."*	So I can just get to work on time.
Bribing: *"I'll place a dollar on the door and the first kid down and ready gets the dollar."*	So we can just get out of here and be on time.
Appeasing: *"I will sit with you while you do your homework tonight, but tomorrow you have to do it by yourself."*	Because I don't want another note from the teacher.
Enabling: *"I will make you another sandwich today, because I know how tired and hungry you are after soccer practice but tomorrow, you will have to do this yourself."*	So we don't have a meltdown in the car and ruin the night.
Taking away: *"I am taking away your video games, because you are just too mean and rude to your brother."*	Because I can't stand it when they fight, I just want it quiet.
Time-out: *"If you take the toy from your sister again, you're going to sit in the time-out spot."*	Because it is annoying to listen to them argue over that stupid toy! He has to know what he is doing is wrong.

Band-Aid	Why Parents Use It
Punishing: *"I will take away your screen time if you are rude to your dad again (or because you didn't do your chores, or you forgot your homework at school again, and so on.)"*	Because I don't have any idea what the heck to do about the rudeness, but if he feels pain, maybe he will stop.
Overlooking: *"I will bring you to the door of your classroom today, but your sister will walk you to the door tomorrow."*	Because I can't stomach another crying bout and we look ridiculous in front of the parents at morning drop-off
Caving and negotiating: *"I will leave the light on tonight, but tomorrow we turn it off so your brother and sister can sleep."*	So we can just get some sleep, I'll do whatever it takes.
Bargaining: *"I will drive you to school today, but tomorrow you have to take the bus."*	So I'll just make life easier and hear less whining.
Saving: *"I'll bring your homework even though you left it on the counter and it's supposed to be your responsibility."*	Because I don't want the teacher to think my kid is a slacker or dumb, and if he gets a zero, he won't make honor roll.
Indulging: *"I'll buy you the candy at the movies this time, but next time you have to bring your own money."*	So you won't melt down in front of everyone; or because I wanted this to be a fun afternoon, and I don't want you to ruin it with a tantrum.
Lecturing: *"I'll drive you to the mall anyway, even though you've been rude and I'll just explain all the ways it's not okay to act like this while on the drive."*	Because I don't want you to be mad at me and make my life worse, and I don't really have the courage to keep you from your friends.

Don't feel badly. I have five children, and I understand sometimes we feel we just "have to" do something. I get that. I hate to be embarrassed as much as the next mom and I like to maintain a sense of peace and harmony in my life. However, I also know that with a constant source of fertilizer to help promote the growth of these pesky weeds, our little rascals are back to their mischief-making in short order. The cycle continues and parents end up discovering at a certain point that they've been taken hostage within the family.

Kids are bargaining, noodling, and eluding their responsibilities, and parents start to live a life they don't enjoy and never envisioned with their children. And I have to tell you, it is not the kids' fault. They did not get here by themselves. By focusing on the short term, using quick fixes, and taking a Band-Aid approach to parenting, parents are creating bad habits and training their kids in the wrong skills, which will continue to make life challenging. More importantly, all of this leads to children who have not had ample time to make mistakes, learn from them, become more independent, take on more responsibilities, work together cooperatively, and develop the mental muscle necessary to better navigate thier own lives and support the health and well-being of their family.

3

Being the Maid:
Doing for Your Kids Is the Problem

Excuse the mess, but we live here.

—*Roseanne Barr*

Never do for a Child, what a Child can do for himself.

—*Rudolf Dreikurs*

If they can walk, they can work.

—*Vicki Hoefle*

In chapter 2 we identified the two types of bullet wounds, training and relationship wounds, and why Band-Aid tactics are ineffective and interfere with the long-term changes you are looking to make. Let's explore how "training" (or the lack thereof) becomes such a major problem for many parents raising kids in today's busy, overscheduled world.

Maybe it started out as a harmless way to help your child keep his life together or get outside to play with his friends or show up prepared for school and sports. Or maybe it started because you are used to order in your life and when the kids were introduced into your world, your responsibilities increased and the family needed your help to stay in sync. Or maybe you have an idea of what it means to be a good parent and what kids of good parents look like, and you set out to accomplish your goal of being a good parent. Whether you landed here accidentally or purposefully, your role as parent has morphed into that of a maid. You are the person who keeps the family together, wipes down the counters, changes the load of laundry, and tidies everything up, household and otherwise. You stop for no one, especially when guests are coming over, the meeting starts at nine in the morning, or you simply can't wait for the rest of the family to get things done. You make "tidy life" materialize for the entire family and there is no coincidence that you are often wiped out by day's end and totally depleted of the joyful energy you envisioned when you started your career as the, well, for lack of a better word, the maid.

Four False Beliefs That Keep the Maid Employed

Parents continue day after day to do for their children what their children can do for themselves because they are driven by four key ideals that either consciously or subconsciously hold them hostage to this occupation as the maid.

1. Kids shouldn't have to work. They will be adults soon enough and they should spend their time enjoying life while they can.
2. Kids will just mess things up. I have high standards, I want things done in a certain way, and the kids could care less.
3. Kids are a reflection of their parents, so it's important that the kids leave the house with their stuff, in clean clothing, and with their lunches in hand.
4. The kids really need me to do things for them.

Fairytale Busted: The Maid Does Not Make Everything Magical

If you're employed as the overworked maid, it's important to stop and identify why you've accepted this job and to look beyond the sparkling surface into how it's affecting everyone in the family. You may think you're creating a "perfect" life for your children, but if you step back, it becomes clear that perhaps being the maid isn't such as good idea. Let's deconstruct the beliefs listed above with a little story to highlight the point that the maid doesn't necessarily make life better by cleaning up everyone's messes.

Belief Number One: *Kids Just Want, and Deserve, to Have Fun*

Many parents hold to the belief that good, loving, (perfect) moms and dads do everything for their kids, so the kids can enjoy their childhood without experiencing the pressures of the adult world. These parents run around serving food, tying shoes, allaying worries, and making life comfortable just to ensure the kids aren't subjected to the stress and strains that come with life. These parents don't mind doing for their kids, despite their own feeling of being overwhelmed; they really believe it's worth it!

Jenny's Exhausting To-Do-for-Them List

At the beginning of my career, before I was even a parent educator, I stayed with a friend whose life goal was to create a space for her children that insulated them from the pressures and responsibilities of the adult world. Here's what I witnessed over the course of a three-day visit. I observed and learned a lot in a very short time!

Jenny, an organized soul, began every morning with a cup of coffee and a list of to-dos for herself and her three kids, in an attempt to make it easy for them to get out of the house on time. Her children slept a little later as she spent the quiet early hours stuffing backpacks, cleaning lunchboxes, and washing stinky soccer clothes in an effort to have everything ready to go. She packed three-food-group-minimum lunches and piled their things on the bench by the door. She untied laces and prepped the place so that all they'd have to worry about was waking, dressing without thinking, eating breakfast, and leaving with their backpacks loaded and ready for another day at school.

I watched her run through her routine, thinking, *That's a lot of work!* But it was just the beginning. On her second cup of coffee, Jenny trotted upstairs to dress for work and get the kids up. I could not see what was going on upstairs, but I could hear every word. It was thirty minutes before any of them made it down the stairs, and the following is just some of what I heard as I sipped my tea.

"Justin [age eight], it's time to get up. I've already turned your alarm off and hit the snooze button for you twice. You are going to have to hurry now, because I let you sleep an extra ten minutes."

"George [age six], it's time to get up. I'll tickle your back for two minutes. See, I am setting the clock. When the alarm goes off you have to promise to get up, okay?" Tick, tick, tick, buzz. "George, I can't tickle you anymore, we are going to be late if you dillydally. I have to get your sister up, George."

"Grace [age four], it's time to get up sleepyhead. I know you hate the mornings, don't you? Let's change your diaper and then we can cuddle for a few minutes. Come on, Grace, your diaper is full and you are getting mommy wet. Please, Grace, how about if you sit on my lap and I will take it off of you while we cuddle? Would you like that?"

In between I heard:

"George, are you dressed? Justin, did you go back to sleep?" And so forth.

Then, the "up-and-at-em" show moved into the kitchen. Nobody was doing much of anything except wandering. The kids weren't being naughty, they just didn't give a hoot that mom was working hard to start their day in joyful comfort. Even after all the preparing and snuggling, the morning was punctuated with whining, crying, pouting, playing, noodling, getting distracted, a bit of hitting, stubbornness, and increasing demands from the kids.

When Jenny finally got the kids in the car and drove away, I went back to bed. I was exhausted. After school, they returned home for a replay, which continued until the kids were in bed. After two more days of this, I asked Jenny bluntly to help me understand this frantic pace she set for herself that had her acting more maid than mom to her kids. She thought about it for a long time, and this is how she summarized her thinking:

Becoming a parent was part of my life plan. I knew that I wanted to be a parent and I had strong ideas of how I would parent, and that included giving my kids a magical childhood. Childhood is supposed to be filled with adventure, excitement, joy, discovery, and a feeling of security. Kids spend the majority of their lives dealing with adult matters. What harm is there in allowing them to enjoy their childhood?

This question, "What's the harm in…?" answered itself over and over through the twenty years I've spent as a parent educator.

Duct Tape Moment

Ask a nice friend who won't think you're nuts to hold the duct tape as you spin around—get those arms down nice and tight. Then have a seat and let your friend tape you to the chair. There is no reason to jump up, do everything, save, and make things "easy" or "perfect" for your child. You can still be a great mom by backing off! Remember, childhood is for learning—and through practice, kids learn skills for the real world. They also develop a solid sense of worth and self-confidence when they don't have their "super mommy" catering to their every move. Give them some room—read a book or go for a run with that spare YOU time!

There's no harm done if:

- You don't mind feeling resentful as you wait on your munchkins.
- You don't mind raising kids who seem oblivious to all that you do for them in order to make their lives more comfortable.
- You don't mind raising kids who believe they are *entitled* to around-the-clock maid service.
- You don't care that your kids won't really know how to run a dishwasher or clothes dryer when they head off to college.
- You don't mind not having any fun as a family because everyone's floundering around with no real responsibility.
- You're willing to take valuable learning away from your kids that will connect them to the world and the community around them.

Ironically, even as Jenny was doing everything for her kids, she was nagging and reminding and *lecturing* them about how *they* should be doing more. It didn't add up. She didn't want to bother the kids by expecting too much or putting them to work, but she did in fact wish they'd magically offer to help out.

This false belief perpetuates a cycle of overwhelmed, over-extended, emotionally unavailable parents. It also delivers to the "real" world ungrateful, overindulged, spoiled children who grow into demanding, dependent, and insecure individuals with little training or experience at handling life's simplest tasks.

It may sound harsh, but my experience shows that children who grow up perfectly protected, catered to, and hovered over are at a complete disadvantage for growth into successful, healthy adults. Maid service offers children little substance or wisdom to draw from later in life, as they discover the world is the opposite of their "perfect" family haven.

Jenny's parting shot to me when I left was, "If you figure out a better way to do this, please let me know." Upon my departure, I spent a great deal of time pondering this dilemma and wondering how I was going to avoid wearing a maid's uniform and feeling resentful in it. This question became a founding principal of my program.

Belief Number Two: I'm Faster, Better, Neater, and a Bit of a Perfectionist, and It's Just Easier If I Do Everything

For many parents, becoming the maid evolves not because they want their kids' lives to be full of magic and wonder, but because they want to drive the car, steer the boat, and fly the plane 365 days of the year. We all know at least one or two moms like this, the strong ones manning the controls because, in their words, if they didn't, the family would most likely crash and burn. I can relate to this personality. I consider myself a reformed control freak. I get the idea that asking a kid to be involved in the running of the house is a sure bet that things won't get done the "right" way (in other words, my way).

My Way or the Highway: Mother Knows Best.

Meet Toni. She's the classic Type A, in charge of everything, mother of two children. She's stern, involved, and, overall, pleasant. You'd say she's that mom who has her act together. She knows what's going on at all times and she makes the final call on just about everything, including the shopping, scheduling, and rule-setting for her family.

Unlike Jenny, who was tiptoeing around, making it easy for the kids with little expectation, Toni is moving fast and furiously with little pushback. Her kids know what their mother wants from them, and they do it. While everyone's eating a balanced breakfast, she's busy choosing clothes for her children, lining up their things by the door, and e-mailing a teacher before class. As the kids finish eating, they run upstairs, throw on their clothes, brush their teeth, and come back down. They pull it off every morning. Toni again is on time, with her coffee cup nestled in the cup holder as they jet off in the minivan. And if anyone forgets anything, she's got a backup plan or can swing home before heading to work!

Toni is also a planner. She recites what the kids are doing after school as she reads them a list of what they will need and where they can find it. Every day, like clockwork, she reminds them to get the water bottle, fill it. Get a snack, bring it. Find your uniform, pack it, and so forth. The kids have little or no say in any of the extracurricular activities they are involved in, but Toni is fair, to a point. She won't force them into every sport or activity, but she believes children need to grow up well-rounded and it is her responsibility to see to it that it happens. There is little negotiation in this arena. This includes birthday parties, school events, and fundraisers. They don't miss anything!

Nutrition is important to her and so is a clean kitchen. If she were to allow her kids into her domain, it would result in pancake-battered, sticky messes! That's not happening, so instead, she's got a neat cabinet system and designated eating areas, because she's not interested in cleaning up messes all over the house. This is not a place Toni is willing to share her time, energy, and space. It gets cluttered and unhealthy stuff creeps in. Inviting her kids into the kitchen (and into the decision-making process) would create an opening for argument, and to her, it's not worth the effort.

Toni also values education and hard work, and she's been known to correct a few assignments in her day. She makes every conference at the school, sends personal notes to the teachers, and logs into the grade portal regularly. She has a special place for the kids to do their homework and makes sure they have all the proper supplies. She's noticed fights stirring about getting homework done, especially as the kids get older and have more to do, but education is important and if she has to demand, threaten, bribe, and lecture them for forty-five minutes, then so be it. Plus, she's not going to let the kids get bad grades, jeopardize their college options, or make the family look as if they didn't know the importance of a good education. This is just not an option.

This Type A maid–mother wears a smile on her face (in public) while giving commands and commenting on nearly every detail of what's going on around her. She doesn't ask, she tells. If the kids try helping out or doing something on their

Duct Tape Moment

Okay, perfectionists, this one will be hard but give it a go! Grab the roll of tape (they make it in pretty colors now, so you can still look fabulous while doing this!) and tape your eyes closed and your mouth shut. This means it's time to refrain from inspecting the effort your kids have made and correcting it to your liking. You'll have no idea if the socks match or the bedroom is spick-and-span. You won't know if the project is glued together perfectly or if a shirt has been worn three times in one week. You must trust that the little details don't matter as much as you think and that kids can make decent decisions—your child may wear his favorite shirt three times this week but it's his preference. Give him your trust and see what happens (that is, after you take off the tape—watch the eyelashes!).

own, she unintentionally micromanages or criticizes. It's usually not long before she wears them down, they quit, and she can do it her way again.

Toni takes this approach (and possibly you do too) not because she's against the kids working hard or helping out, but because she doesn't want to experience the mess and errors that come with training and inviting the kids to help. Involving the kids more sounds good in theory, and she's thinking, "Maybe I should be letting the kids do more for themselves and be involved around the house, but I like things a certain way and it's just easier to do it myself. I have a routine, a system that works for me. Plus, I'm a perfectionist. My kids will never get it right, so why put us all through that? Is there something wrong with everyone just trusting me and getting through the day as I've planned?"

There's nothing wrong if:

- You aren't worried about sending your son out into the world with little or no training on how to navigate tasks and make choices that work for him (not you).
- You aren't concerned he'll accept direction from people who are "in charge" regardless of whether they have his best interest in mind ("Do this because I say so, okay, little boy?").
- You won't be surprised when he decides that he will never be controlled again and sets out to ensure this by instead controlling others.
- You don't mind raising a child who lacks the confidence to try new things and take reasonable risks and who never develops his own unique set of preferences, styles, routines, and solutions.
- You don't mind telling your child every day (through your actions) that you don't trust him to make decisions, perform tasks, or accept responsibility for his work and choices (because you're doing things he can do, but won't let him try!).
- You don't mind the increase in fighting between your kids and between you and the kids because they don't have anything more interesting/substantial to do.

Parents in this cycle readily overlook the increase in fighting, power struggles, discord, resentment, and disconnection at the expense of a clean house and prompt schedule created by an accomplished maid. Essentially, the message is: If everything's done my way right now, so what if my child is upset with me? He's dressed appropriately and his room is clean.

The truth is, this belief perpetuates a cycle of overbearing, overpowering, micromanaging parenting that leaves little room for the kids to learn how to navigate their own lives, contribute in positive ways, and feel valued by their parents. In turn, the kids feel useless and undermined and start to make mischief. The mother who does everything for the child turns her child into a young adult who can't do anything for himself. This is clearly not what parents intend when they put on that uniform.

Belief Number Three: If My Kids Don't Look Good, Behave Politely, Play Fair, and Do the Right Thing All the Time, I'll Look Like a Slacker Parent with Loser Kids

Here we have the parents who pick up the apron because they believe that their children are extensions and reflections of them. These parents are interested in looking composed, clean, and put together and will sacrifice individuality to avoid public error and to keep a polished exterior. This may sound superficial, although it's not necessarily. Many parents say they feel judged as good or bad parents by how good or bad the kids are in public.

My Kids Are My Image: Make Mother Look Good

Meet Katie. Katie's just as busy as Jenny and Toni are. She runs around cleaning and sweeping and wiping and saving and making excuses and letting kids off the hook because she thinks if her kids are messy or her house is dirty, her friends might consider her a neglectful parent!

I met Katie in a workshop, where she admitted she did everything in her house and she was wiped out. When I asked what prompted her to take on the role of maid, she said, "I am being judged as a parent based on how my kids look, behave, how well they do in school and on the sports field, whether they are respectful to adults and cooperate when asked. I am even being judged based on whether my kids say please and thank you, and that's only the half of it."

Katie believed her kids had to look good, sound good, and be good, her home had to be organized and orderly, and her life needed to reflect that she was on top of everything in order to consider herself a good mom. "My kids and my home define me." That was the fear that pushed her to drive herself into the ground, worrying about everything from neat and tidy jeans to clean toilets to matching socks.

When I spent one-on-one time with Katie, I noticed she was on high alert, watching for what the kids might do that needed correcting. She was monitoring to make sure she didn't need to step in and redirect, straighten a shirt, prompt a replay, or give "the look." Katie was so concerned with how people would judge her that she orchestrated everything she could in her children's lives so that none of them would look foolish, ill-prepared, lazy, or unintelligent. Her value as a mom was essentially tied up in how other people rated her and how well the kids measured up.

When I asked Katie what she thought of letting go and caring a bit less about what everyone else thought of her as a mother, she said, "I would love to let go a little, but I just can't risk my kids being 'that family' with their ends unraveled. It can't hurt to keep a good image, because it will only help them down the road."

I thought of all the parents I'd met over the years who worked so hard to please the outside world. If this were really what good parenting was about it would make sense, but it's not and it doesn't. Katie and I discussed the following points.

Duct Tape Moment

Cover the peephole to the outside world. It doesn't matter what's going on out there or who will be waiting on the front porch, at the school, or in your church or community to judge you. Then, cover your ears and secure your feet. You don't need to be so worried that everything your kids say will embarrass you or tarnish the family's image. Stop listening for what to correct or rephrase! Let them discuss, chat, argue, tell you "no" if they're really against something (it's good practice for the real world), and have a say in who they like or don't like.

Once you stop listening for what's wrong, you'll stop stepping in and redirecting your children in the direction that makes you look best. The outside world will not be there in twenty-five years when your child returns home to visit you for the holidays. The relationship comes first because it'll eventually be just you and your family at the table—none of the rest will have mattered.

It can't hurt if:

- You think kids are possessions, not individuals who have a right to develop and grow and create their own preferences and personalities (even if they like less "upstanding" activities).
- It won't bother you when your teen rebels, sending a very clear message she could care less about your image.
- You aren't concerned that your kids care more about what others think and less about how they view themselves as individuals.

- You aren't worried that your kids will become critical and judgmental of those people who do not care about their image.
- You want to drive home a message that who your kids are right now isn't "good enough" and will understand when they seek out others who treat them the same way in a relationship.
- You don't care that your kid senses you're trying to make her into "the perfect child," something fake, something she's not.
- You're okay with having your kids lose their spunk and enthusiasm for life because they view themselves as trophy kids and base their value on whether they make you look good.
- You don't mind having your child describe you as an overbearing mother who cared more about her own image than she did about the self-image her daughter was developing.

Parents who believe this myth are so caught up in looking good that they lose sight of what's really important: investing themselves in the life they are creating with their children and the memories that will define them as a family. Life with kids is about accepting that kids and parents make mistakes, and mistakes make all of us look a bit messy around the edges. And yes, it's true, showing up for life and all it has to offer can sometimes expose our flaws to the world. It also offers parents a chance to teach their kids about resilience, acceptance, and choosing family over an image.

Belief Number Four: I Don't Want My Child to Grow Up and Not Want Me around, So I'll Just Make Sure She Needs Me Enough

And finally, there are parents who need to be needed by their children and think that the best way to ensure they are needed is to keep their kids completely dependent on them for as long as they can, in as many areas as they can.

Mommy Needs to Be Needed

Joan is a mother of one. When I first met her, she didn't really identify with the other beliefs, but when she got here, she knew right away why she did everything for her child. She shared this with the class:

I've just had an aha moment! I figured it out! I know why I do everything. It's all about me! I didn't even think about Ava, my daughter. I do all this so I feel needed. I'm involved in everything, whether she technically needs me or not. I thought I was doing her favors and making our bond stronger, but I see that I haven't been doing that at all. I am the maid to give myself a job that makes me feel valuable and important, and as a way to keep my child close to me, but parenting isn't about me. It's not necessary that my nine-year-old still depends on me to pour her cereal in the morning, to help her get herself up and out of the door on time, to organize her closets and pick out her clothes. It's not necessary, and it certainly isn't good for her to look to me for constant direction and to make every decision about her life. It is time that she do this without believing that she needs her mommy! I have to stop asking her if she wants help all the time. I'm guessing she doesn't! I never thought it was a big deal to be in her space all the time, but now I get it.

In this moment, I knew that she was on her way to redefining her role as a parent.

It's only a big deal if:

- You want your child to feel shackled because of her mom's need to be needed.
- You're looking forward to the rebellion that is sure to come as your child cuts the ties and distances herself from you.
- Your purpose is to raise a child too scared to try anything without parental assistance.
- You're up for raising an extreme risk taker who makes dangerous choices in order to gain some kind of control in his life.
- You're okay with a child who'll sabotage her own success to keep mom happy.
- You can accept that your child will find a replacement for you once she outgrows her dependency on her mother.
- You are looking forward to the insecurities and frustrations of your child down the road.
- You don't mind needing to help support your twenty-something with her basic needs, even though she's well capable.

In this case, there's nothing more to say. Mom is the maid because it makes *her* feel important; it has absolutely nothing to do with the child's needs. This is the easiest belief to recognize and also one of the easiest to stop, once you realize that you're not doing an ounce of good by tethering your child through her formative years!

If Kids Don't Want a Maid, What *Do* They Want?

Here's a simple list for you to go back to when you realize you're working as the maid! It'll help you remember why it's a good idea to take off the maid uniform and instead invite your kids to participate more fully in their own lives.

1. Kids want to be self-sufficient.

    From the moment our kids arrive on the planet, one of their primary goals is to become self-sufficient. They let us know this with "I can do it" or "I don't need your help" and all of that pushback. It's not about you. It's about your child becoming self-sufficient, which is something that won't happen if you're always doing everything! When this drive is interrupted, children become discouraged and frustrated. Not to mention, it affects their self-esteem, which is based on two factors: (a) their ability to take care of basic needs and (b) their ability to contribute in positive ways to the group (in this case, the family). Take these two opportunities away and you have a discouraged kid who's ready to make mischief and cause trouble!

2. Kids want to feel capable.

    Believe it or not, kids are just like adults. They *want* to feel like they are capable of handling life. This means, at the simplest level, to take care of their basic needs. That includes getting up in the morning, picking out clothes, choosing what to eat for breakfast, and deciding what snack to bring to school and what to pack in their lunch. When kids feel less than capable, they begin to *act* as if they are less than capable. You know, the "I can't do it, you do it for me" drill. Then you do it and it isn't exactly what they wanted or how they wanted and a fight ensues. The more you can learn to omit yourself from their daily tasks, the more independent they grow and the more willing they are to take on greater responsibility.

3. Kids want ownership.

When you do things for children that they can do for themselves, kids begin to think it's your job to do everything. If you don't do it all, you become the focus of their blame, rage, and frustration. The kids don't enjoy this any more than you do, but they become frustrated that you let this happen to them and that they aren't able to do these things themselves. A third grader may blame you and cause a fight because you forgot to pack snow pants, but he's also probably wondering why he can't be in charge of his own stuff. However, the expectation that "mom will do it for me" keeps kids in this idle, angry place. If they had to be responsible and take more ownership, they would have less reason to blame you and at the same time gain more experience to build confidence.

Here is a recap of the faulty beliefs that get us into trouble:

- Mother makes it easy.
- Mother knows best.
- Mother looks good.
- Mother needs to be needed.

Perhaps you believe a bit of each of these. Take some time and make your own list of the things that influence your decision to keep wearing that uniform. Is it a messy house or a fear of looking disorganized? Is it that you want things done your way or that you have no other purpose? This will help you discover some good information when you get to the next section and get to throw in the towel and *quit your job as the maid.*

4

Holding onto Discipline: Your Fear Is the Problem

FEAR is an acronym in the English language for
'False Evidence Appearing Real.'
—Neale Donald Walsch

When you are making parenting decisions out of fear,
you are not parenting in the best interest of your child.
—Vicki Hoefle

In chapter 3 we addressed the training bullet wound and identified how parents spend time trying to Band-Aid behaviors with quick-fix strategies instead of identifying the real problem: kids are not being trained to take care of their basic needs and participate effectively and willingly within the family. Now we will take a look at the relationship bullet wound, which until this point has disguised itself as children requiring more discipline.

The Beginning of Your Family

Before the children arrive, couples everywhere dream about what it will be like to become new parents and how they will go about raising their amazing children. It's such an exciting time.

I'm sure you remember all the time you spent imagining life with your child and all the promises you made about how life would be for you and your baby. No screaming, yelling, or punishing from you. You would be a calm, confident, loving, nurturing parent who would guide your child through the ins and outs of life with the kind of ease that can only be admired. You and your child would create a special bond together, making it possible for you to cooperate and show respect for each other with no power struggles or disrespect from either party. You would provide your child with freedom without giving up your own.

Parents know what they want for themselves and for their kids, and they have a vision for what life will be like when their children arrive. They want each day to be filled with love, laughter, connection, and learning and to make memories with their kids that will last a lifetime. They want to feel the same connection with their nine-year-old that they felt when they held their newborn, and they want to be a guiding force in their teen's life rather than being on opposite sides of every issue. They want to get out of the house on time without any fighting or nagging and to talk at the dinner table and reconnect as a family after a busy day away from each other.

Parents want to know, with some certainty, that their kids are capable of making decisions, taking responsibility for themselves, and making amends. Parents want to feel like they are their kids' allies, their champions and cheerleaders, and they want to feel respected and appreciated in their own homes. Parents want time to enjoy life with their kids and to maintain their own lives. It's clear that these dreams, desires, and visions for parenting are heavily weighted in creating and maintaining a loving, respectful, and fulfilling relationship with our kids.

Unfortunately for many parents, when this vision of parental bliss doesn't materialize and their once easy-to-please one-year-old is replaced with a demanding, screeching two-year-old, parents begin to employ an assortment of tactics to "force" their real child into becoming the dream child they planned to raise. This is where the vision of parenting (great relationships in family life) collides with the reality of raising an actual child with a unique personality. Parents are suddenly preoccupied with finding any tools, techniques, strategies, or approaches that might bring back the dream, the vision, and the bliss they dreamed about having.

This is where, unknowingly, the focus of our parenting journey shifts away from developing the relationship with the kids and toward finding a discipline strategy to "get the kids" to act in accordance with our ideas of parenting. We don't even realize we're shifting our focus in an effort to get to what we want out of family life. Once we've jumped onto the discipline track, it steers us away from our original dreams of family life and into a cycle of employing Band-Aid tactics to control the kids, their behavior, and their daily lives. That's why it's so important to recognize when things get off track and to understand that there are solutions—real common sense solutions—that will put us back in touch with those initial dreams and refocus our attention back on building the relationship with our kids. So, what happens to make us switch from investing in the relationship with our kids to searching for discipline strategies to control them?

There are four basic fears that parents live with that cause them to hold on to a discipline approach to parenting rather than a relationship approach to parenting.

Fear Number One: Not Addressing Kids' Bad Behavior Means Mom and Dad Become the Doormat

If this is your fear, you may have already decided that there is *no* way that your child is going to run the roost. You worked hard to get where you are and no little kids, even squishy-faced cute ones, are going to have you jumping through hoops while they act like spoiled brats.

Or perhaps you're afraid of the hairy eyeball from strangers. You don't want to go through the day with kids running loose and hear the opinions of onlookers who think you need to do something with that kid of yours. So you keep the reins tight, just in case.

You're committed to never, ever becoming a permissive parent. And so it sounds great to back off of discipline and focus on the relationship until the kids make a ruckus in public. Then, well, there you go, right back to the Band-Aid tactics and other interfering discipline strategies.

In 1999, a mother in one of my classes who was right in the middle of this fear, raised her hand and said, "I see the reasoning in what you are saying. My problem is this: when I think of relationship strategies, I imagine my kids running the house and I can't see where that would be any more beneficial than me running the house." We all shared a collective laugh. Good point. She is afraid of becoming the doormat, not even to her fuzzy-headed four-year-old.

This mom, like so many others, equates relationship strategies with permissive parenting. She's not interested in being a doormat, not even to a four-year-old. Her goal—to maintain control and order—is fair, based on her fear. And since she has never trusted that her kids "helping out around the house" could actually be a good idea, filled with cooperation, order, and responsibility, she has no reason to give that fear up.

Let's freeze this thought for just a minute and reflect on how adult relationships work.

As adults, our best functional relationships are balanced. Nobody feels like the doormat and nobody feels like the dictator. I'm not saying unbalanced relationships don't exist for adults, but they're probably not the ones we enjoy or are involved with for long. In balanced relationships, boundaries are established early on. There is a give and take for respecting personal preferences and the focus is on enjoying each other's company, supporting each other as individuals, and valuing a different perspective. You accommodate for personality (yes, your friend may run late, but you love him anyway) and you negotiate solutions (you can't afford that girls' weekend away, but you can meet for dinner downtown).

The point is, you'd never force a friend to change or behave in accordance with what you consider a more appropriate manner because either you are willing to overlook the differences in your personalities and preferences or you know she'd walk, and click "unfriend" on the way out. You also know that if you don't hold up your end of the relationship by investing in the health of it, it will start to fizzle, and you don't want that so you stay tuned in. The big picture is always on the relationship, even if you have bumpy patches, not on the day-to-day details.

And if you're thinking, Gee, well, my kid is not supposed to be my friend, consider that I am simply suggesting that you establish mutually respectful boundaries and that family members learn to accept each other's tiny faults. I am advocating that you accept that everyone is working hard to be her best in any given situation, and not that you chum around with your seven-year-old. I am here to tell you that it is possible to parent your child while treating her like you would a treasured friend, creating a perfect balance of mutual respect, love, tolerance, and guided direction when necessary.

Relationship strategies don't suggest that parents roll over and give unstructured, at-random control of the house to the kids or give up on raising children with moral character and values.

Relationship strategies do suggest that we, as parents, do not have an automatic right to force kids to live their lives in accordance with our preferences. Just because we can't stand the thought of a messy room doesn't mean we have to spend an exhausting amount of energy trying to get a child who could care less to keep it spotless. Indeed, there is a middle point, a balanced system of give and take that supports each member of the family and the family as a whole.

Children are trying to figure out who they are, what they like, and how they want to navigate the world around them. Parents who provide children with opportunities to develop their own preferences and take ownership of their own lives can hardly be considered pushovers. It's a matter of establishing a respectful relationship and allowing children to unfold, to develop, to grow, and to change. If we invite our children to be the kids they are, instead of forcing them to be the kids we demand, we will certainly see them show up and participate more willingly and with more enthusiasm within the family. Similarly, if we invest in the relationship we have with our kids when they are young, we will most certainly receive an invitation to participate in their lives when they enter adolescence and then leave our homes for their solo journeys into the world. I'll show you how easy and fun this can be. Just hang on and keep reading.

Fear Number Two: If the Kid Doesn't Feel Bad, He's Not Learning a Lesson

If you are a parent who really believes that people, including children, can only learn if they suffer just a bit, then a strategy that focuses on teaching a lesson (even if it's a bit harsh) is your first response when you feel you have to "do something."

Example number one: Your seven-year-old daughter is rude to a friend from school and you want her to understand that it's not okay to treat people that way. So, in addition to the natural consequence (the friend not playing with your child, which may or may not happen this time—or ever), you drive home a series of punishments, anything from taking away cherished items to lecturing and guilt-tripping her into feeling like she did a really lousy thing and that only bad kids act that way. Your goal is to add the sting of screwing up to teach the lesson.

Example number two: Your five-year-old son has started pushing his two-year-old brother down if the little one comes too close to his Legos. The next time you see him do it, you lecture him on keeping his hands to himself, tell him you are putting the Legos away for three days, and that he can go to time-out and think about what he did.

Example number three: Your six-year-old daughter is caught playing with your iPhone without permission. You give her a fierce lecture on using your things without permission and take one of her favorite toys away from her to teach her a lesson.

First and foremost, understand that the learning process is interrupted in children (and adults) when fear, uncertainty, and stress are added to the situation. When this happens, humans retreat inward out of self-preservation, and the ability to learn and discern stops. The child is not capable of making the connection between his behavior moments ago and the lesson you want him to learn once you start to use punishment and verbal lashings to drive the point home. The "lesson" is lost, and the only thing loud and clear is the voice telling the child how bad he is, how he has let someone down, and how he will never get it right. The learning—which was intended to be a message to treat friends better, keep your hands to yourself, or to ask before you take—has stopped. It has evaporated, and what has settled in its place for the child is a residual sense of worthlessness.

Clearly, a parent who believes that feeling bad is necessary to achieve proper behavior in kids is going to have a tough time making the decision to invest in a suite of relationship strategies. But if the primary goal is to teach, then why not use

Duct Tape Moment

The next time you feel the urge to "teach a lesson," skip it. Pull out the tape and cover your mouth. The well-intended point will evaporate in the delivery and the child will carry away feelings residual of worthlessness. It doesn't mean you don't care, it just means you're choosing to react in a positive way over a negative way. Attempting to teach a lesson in a moment of anger or lashing out because "She can't get away with this!" will never work when you're heated, upset, emotional, or defensive. All the child will hear is a familiar voice telling her how bad she is, how she has let someone down, and how she will never get it right. You have to keep your mouth shut until you've cooled off and you can revisit the incident in a positive light.

one of the world's best teachers, natural consequences. Natural consequences come up in class all the time, and if you're afraid of switching your focus to the relationship, it's helpful to get a good definition and understanding of the power of nature. You can eliminate your fear entirely if you understand how natural consequences work and that your child will, in fact, learn without you ever opening your mouth.

A natural consequence is the result of a behavior, habit, mishap, or "oopsy" with absolutely no involvement or interference from the parents. Natural consequences happen whether you, the parent, are present or not, and they happen whether you want them to happen or not. Here's where we can use a classic example: it's twenty-eight degrees outside and the child leaves his hat at home.

- It's cold out.
- Brian leaves hat at home.
- Brian is cold at recess.
- Brian does not like the feeling.
- Brian remembers hat the next day.
- Or perhaps he'll borrow a hat.
- Or maybe he'll wear a t-shirt over his ears.
- It doesn't matter because the child will figure something out.

That's it. That's the lesson, and nature will teach it once or a hundred times without any emotional investment in whether the child has a cold noggin at recess or not.

Often, parents want to rush the experience or they feel like they need to make it stick with an "I told you so" to anchor the lesson. But the kids don't need it! Kids get it loud and clear, as long as mom doesn't rush to bring him a hat and then lecture! We've all seen that, right?

So, if you ever find yourself in a place where you want to "teach a lesson," but you think you'd like to choose the relationship, remember that the world is set up to help your child learn lessons with nearly every event, decision, and mistake. The daily grind of life offers kids countless golden opportunities to learn with no emotional attachment to what's going on. Sometimes kids get away with it. Other times, it takes a long time to harvest the natural response to a behavior, like losing friends over being bossy or mean. Either way, you can't "teach" something by adding a bite in the bottom. Think of the last time someone tried to teach you a lesson by acting like a jerk. Did you learn a bit of wisdom or did you walk away feeling disconnected and low? Use what's readily available and it'll help take the pressure off both you and your child and allow for a better connection between the two of you.

Duct Tape Moment

Use as much tape as you need and tape as many body parts as you must to stay out, let go, stop from jumping in, sit back, keep quiet, and refrain from saving your child from discomfort. Natural consequences are everywhere and are built in to the daily grind—you have to trust these natural lessons and let kids discover how the real world will react to their decisions and behaviors.

If your child is bossy, you can't step in, correct, lecture, and explain how she'll have no friends. You have to stay out and let her lose a friend, or perhaps discover that kids will stand up to her and she'll have to change if she wants to keep her friends. Or maybe she's funny and likeable and the bossiness isn't a big deal with her friends. You can't teach a lesson that is not yours to teach—and when a child learns a lesson the hard way, it's not okay to peel back the tape for an old-fashioned "I told you so." It's her lesson, let her learn it without your commentary.

Fear Number Three: My Kids Are Hooligans, and If I Back Off They Will Get Totally Out of Control

At a 2008 workshop I facilitated, a parent stood up and shared with the group, "Children need to be disciplined. That is how they learn. Without discipline they will be out of control. I am not going to raise or live with an out-of-control child!" Her remarks were met with applause from the audience.

"Okay," I said to my workshop participants, "can you give me some examples of things your kids do that require you to use discipline in order for them to learn and to keep them from getting 'out of control'?"

A parent replied, "Sure. I have a list of things. When my kids:

- Fight with each other
- Refuse to get up and get ready in the morning
- Disrupt the family at dinner time
- Leave their toys thrown all over the house
- Come into my room and wake me up a hundred times a night
- Use a sassy, disrespectful tone with me
- Disobey the rules
- Can't remember their stuff and make us late"

The parent continued, "I feel like I have to discipline them in order to keep the day moving and under control."

I stopped her there and said, "From my perspective, nothing on this list constitutes a discipline problem. In my mind, these fall into two categories: they are either lack of training problems or fractured relationship problems, and both types are easy to solve."

The mother's jaw dropped and I continued, "I'd like to ask everyone in the audience a few questions. Raise your hands if you have used a specific discipline technique more than ten times to deal with one specific problem and maintain control of the kids and the house. This includes daily doses of nagging, reminding, lecturing, counting, time-outing, bribing, and saving, all standard parenting strategies for controlling behavior."

One hundred and twenty hands shot up.

"Keep your hand up if you have used the strategy more than twenty times."

One hundred and twenty hands stayed up.

"Keep your hands up if you believe that there is any possibility that using the same strategy another twenty times, fifty times, or a hundred times will cause the problem to disappear."

There was a long pause. And then the hands began to drop. Five hands stayed up. I counted.

"Here is my last question: raise your hand if this is how you want to spend time with your kids."

Not one hand went up.

The fear of losing control leads parents to overuse ineffective discipline strategies and Band-Aid tactics to control kids, which in turn has the opposite effect on the children. The more times a parent employs one of these techniques, the more "out of control" the kids seem to be, especially when the parent is not around. There also seems to be an increase in fighting and power struggles between family members, not a lessening of them. The more focus there is on controlling the kids so they "do what they are supposed to do," the less positive connection there is between parents and their children. This interferes with the ability to develop strong, loving, respectful relationships.

Parents *must* be ready to walk away from the paralyzing idea that their children will become out-of-control hooligans if they are not under constant surveillance. I understand the desire for order, for routines, and for respectful kids. But the mentality held by many parents today who believe all little people are destined to turn into out-of control monsters if a parent doesn't clamp down on them is just too far-fetched. In fact, when I listen to parents divulge their fear stories, I find myself wondering who in the world they are talking about. Surely not that towheaded four-year-old, highly engaged seven-year-old, introspective nine-year-old, socially sophisticated thirteen-year-old, or determined sixteen-year-old I met at school or in my home! And I bet you've experienced this same confusion. A parent comes to you with what seems to her like an end-of-the-world story about her six-year-old and you giggle or shrug it off because you know the child and you know he is most certainly not out of control, a hooligan, or a jerk when he is around you and other adults. If we can think like this about our own kids, a lot of the stress begins to fade.

If you see yourself here, write down exactly what out of control would look like to you. There's no right or wrong. Perhaps as you scribble down all the worst-case scenarios, you'll see that they might just be stories in your head. Most of the time, it is fear that creeps in and sticks, even though it is really just nonsense. Obviously some fears are valid, but if you write everything down, at least you'll see true concerns versus hyped-up fiction in your brain.

Fear Number Four: My Relationship Strategies Simply Won't Work

In class, when I ask what relationship strategies parents are using, the list often includes:

- Reading with the kids
- Spending time doing fun things with the kids
- Playing games with the kids
- Snuggling with the kids

These are not relationship strategies. These are the ways we spend quality time with our kids. This is part of the confusion that cranks up this fear. These strategies won't work as relationship strategies because they aren't! Relationship strategies go beyond just hanging out and playing with the kids because we love them. Relationship strategies take time to set up and they are not reactive to the situation of the moment.

They are designed to:

- Create healthy habits
- Develop routines that support all family members

- Teach children problem-solving techniques
- Demonstrate respectful communication
- Distribute family work equitably
- Handle squabbles between siblings
- Create realistic expectations for behavior
- Instill purpose and value for all family members
- Model values and behaviors
- Deepen and strengthen relationships between all family members

The relationships we enjoy most are cooperative, supportive, respectful, loving, empathetic, and understanding. When challenges arise, we find ways to work things out. We talk, we listen, we brainstorm, we disagree, we compromise, we agree, and we move forward. In other words, we invest deeply in our most important relationships and we are open to changing in order to keep the relationship healthy. And maybe more importantly than that, we accept the other person in the relationship for who they are, with an understanding that they too are in the process of growing and changing.

Finding the balance between maintaining a strong, healthy relationship with our kids, helping them become independent, thinking, responsible, resilient people, creating powerful memories of love and connection, and maintaining order in a respectful and manageable way can be tricky, but I guarantee you that it is possible, that it can be a fun and exciting journey, and that it is worth every moment of uncertainty.

More than any of the other solutions I'll share with you in the following chapters, the foundation for a strong, respectful, fulfilling relationship with your children is determined by the emphasis you put on implementing relationship strategies and setting aside your desire to manage, punish, or control.

5

The Cul-de-Sac Syndrome: Your Thinking Is the Problem

Your own best thinking got you here.
—*Bill Wilson, Alcoholics Anonymous*
Twelve-Step Program

The problem with any parenting strategy isn't necessarily the strategy itself, but the thinking a parent applies to implementing the strategy.
—*Vicki Hoefle*

By now, you understand that feeding the weed, using Band-Aid tactics, doing too much for your kids, and fearing an investment in the relationship has you going round and round in a parenting cul-de-sac. You've discovered that, even though you know you aren't going anywhere, you stay with your foot on the pedal, driving by the same scenario over and over and over again, scratching your head and wondering what to do. And once you're at the end of your rope, you set off to find another strategy to get your kids to behave, be nice, be good, be respectful, be responsible, pick up their toys, hang up their jackets, clear their plates, keep their hands off their brother, drop the sass, do their homework, and so on.

You've witnessed firsthand that the strategy you employed

on Monday to combat those big, beefy misbehaviors fizzled out by Wednesday because it just didn't "fix" the problem. You may take a step forward but then there are always a few steps back. Instead of life with the kids getting easier and more enjoyable, life seems to get more complicated, hostile, micromanaged, and uncooperative. It's not at all what you envisioned but there's no clear path to the right direction.

Despite a rotation of strategies and techniques, reactions and plans, there is one constant in this round and round commotion: your thinking. If you're not willing to rethink your thinking then it won't matter how many strategies you employ. You're set on a course for more of the same. From now on, it's important to remember this key point: a *new* strategy is *not* new thinking.

The Thinking That Keeps Us Going Around and Around

Let's take a moment to reflect on where you, as well meaning and caring parents, tend to get snagged and set in a cycle of ineffective parenting. To do this, we'll review briefly some of what we covered in chapters 1 through 4.

In chapter 1, we identified that your thinking was grounded in getting rid of all those pesky behaviors your children exhibit in any given situation. You didn't realize your laser focus and constant attention to the problem were the fertilizer that fed the very weeds you were trying to eradicate from your garden.

Your thinking, which had a goal of "making it stop," resulted in micromanaging, nagging, reminding, lecturing, yelling, punishing, bribing, and saving your kids in an attempt to put a stop to behaviors ranging from naughty to annoying to inconvenient. But no matter how much focus you put on trying to get rid of those behaviors, nothing changed. Why? Because your thinking was always the same: the more effort I put into getting this behavior to stop, the faster it will stop!

The result of this "feed the weed" cycle? Your focus was misplaced and you were actually feeding the very behaviors and attitudes in your children that were driving you crazy! In your attempt to find a reprieve from the weeds, you let them take over your daily life. You thought the behavior was the focus, not the relationship, and you got more of what you did not want.

In chapter 2, your thinking landed you in reactive mode, using Band-Aid tactics with a short-sighted view and a desire to just keep the family moving forward through the day, no matter what the cost, and with no thought for the long-term damage.

Your thinking had you giving in, making concessions, using scare tactics, and jumping from one confusing strategy to another in the hope that you could get some traction in your day and make it till bedtime without blowing a gasket. You found yourself in a back-and-forth approach to discipline, rules, routines, and so forth. You perpetuated this power shifting because your thinking about what was most important never changed. There has got to be a strategy to deal with this and I will find it if it kills me!

The result? Your use of Band-Aid tactics and ping-pong approaches to parenting had everyone in the family confused, frustrated, and working against each other. You discovered that there is very little cooperation within the family and that your tactics headed everyone further into discouragement rather than making things better.

In chapter 3, your thinking landed you in a thankless, non-stop job as maid because it was easier, faster, you could do the tasks better, and the kids don't really care about helping out anyway. Unfortunately, your role as a parent took a backseat and the family began to suffer.

Your thinking had you either doing everything for the kids or devising complicated systems for coaxing their cooperation, micromanaging them to ensure things were done correctly and to your liking, or threatening them with loss of privileges if they didn't get with the program and pull their weight. Your thinking had you believing that it was your job to make sure everyone was doing everything correctly and on time, all the time, and that the kids couldn't or wouldn't help out in a consistent manner even if you asked them. You voluntarily kept all the balls juggled in the air so that life could run more smoothly. Your thinking about what good moms do and what good families look like didn't change—only your approach changed. You stayed in that uniform because your thinking never changed: the kids won't help, and if they do help it will be a mess so I will take care of it and everyone will be happy.

The result was that you found yourself doing too much for the kids. You realized that acting more like maid than mom left you emotionally depleted, exhausted, and resentful from doing too much, and the kids were becoming more demanding and discouraged with each passing day.

In chapter 4, your fears that investing in relationship strategies would lead to chaos and permissive parenting had you on the prowl for more creative and punitive discipline strategies, which only caused further fractures in the family atmosphere.

This thinking had you believing that you had to keep a firm hold, maintain control, and teach a hard lesson or everything would fall apart. You didn't trust yourself to invest in your relationship with your kids because it would mean you were a permissive parent, and everyone knows what happens in a permissive home. You steered clear of relationship-building strategies because your thinking made it impossible to even consider them. You don't think there is any way you can raise kids using relationship strategies.

The result? Your fears that investing in relationship strategies would turn you into a pushover parent and your uncertainty about what really qualified as a relationship strategy wouldn't let you consider them as viable parenting options. You found yourself caught up in the drive to "do something," so you paid attention to everything, which led to more discord, not less.

Parents stay in these cycles because they don't know how or where to get new information that will lead them in the right direction. They don't know that if they step out of the drama or ignore certain behaviors, the relationship will improve. If our thinking is influenced by idealism, limited by expectation, filled with worst-case scenarios, or overly focused on what others think, our ability to parent with intention and clarity is impaired. We blindly resort to an over-parenting style that only complicates our efforts to achieve a happy, cooperative family.

New Information, New Thinking

If what you really want is a loving, cooperative, and trusting relationship with your children and a warm, loving atmosphere to raise them in, then the first thing you have to do is get accurate information about what's really going on in your home. That new information is what changes our thinking and, in turn, changes the family.

This means we have to be honest and ask ourselves, Do I really believe that:

- A child who says "shut up" will grow up to be a delinquent who is disrespectful to everyone?

- Keeping a clean house is an indication of how much I love my kids?
- A child will become a problem child if I don't correct every misbehavior?
- It's critically important to have a "good" kid who never loses his temper or raises his voice?
- Daily sibling spats add up to obnoxious, out-of-control, and rude teens?

In all cases, the answer is no, none of this nonsense is as horrible as we tend to make it. Our rational selves understand that the only thing that really matters is our relationship with our children. But if we let limited thinking about discipline determine and dictate the daily interactions with our children, we lose our ability to step outside the moment and recognize the big picture.

To change our thinking, we have to have the courage to admit that it needs changing:

- *My child's attitude is not the problem.* My demanding that it change is the problem.
- *The whining is not the problem.* My focus on it is the problem.
- *The tantrums are not the problem.* My participation in them is the problem.
- *The morning chaos is not the problem.* Lack of training is the problem.
- *My child acting out is not the problem.* Thinking her naughty behavior makes me look bad is the problem.
- *My child's lack of cooperation is not the problem.* My criticizing and correcting him is the problem.
- *My child not listening isn't the problem.* My demands are the problem.

- *My child's bad habits aren't the problem.* My judgment of them is the problem.

And following up on this change in thinking with some strong, rational affirmations can make all the difference in your success:

- I will let go of what's not working.
- Change happens over time.
- Focus on the progress and improvement and forget the rest.
- I am hung up on details I won't remember in ten years.
- I am investing in my child's emotional health.
- A three-year-old's tantrum doesn't define me as a parent.
- I have what it takes to wait this out.
- If I wait five minutes and show some faith, this will blow over.
- I know what won't work in the long run, and I choose *not* to do it.
- I am going to trust my child with that outfit, decision, preference, or emotion.
- I'm not interested in getting involved anymore.
- If it's not morally or physically dangerous, I'm willing to stay out.
- I might not like it but I'll let him try it.
- The goal is to say yes.
- I believe my kids can do more than I let them try.
- How they act does not make me a good or bad mother.
- Thinking, curious kids are messy.
- Engaged kids take reasonable risks.
- Confident kids reach out.
- Resilient kids overcome frustrations, embarrassment, rejection, and failure.

All of this might seem overwhelming (or even crazy at first read), but trust me, if you can take a minute and let this information settle in, I promise that as you read the next section of solutions you will open up to what is possible for you as a parent and a person, and for what is possible for your family.

To be clear, this change in thinking does not mean you suddenly let your kids off the hook just because you can admit that what you are doing now might not be helping the situation. A better relationship is built on more accountability from both you and your child. What this does mean is that you can admit that what you're doing isn't working and that, perhaps, some of the mountains you make are nothing more than molehills.

Your Turn: Crack Open
Your Thinking about Parenting

Now it's your turn to see what you really think about parenting.

Part one: Get a pen and write down all the problem areas you are facing in your family. Make a list. This list could include anything from dinnertime meltdowns to homework difficulties to sibling rivalry. Write up a beefy list, so you have lots to think about.

Part two: Now describe these situations in more detail.

- Mornings—the kids aren't getting up without four reminders each, they refuse to get dressed without me sitting with them or won't wear the clothes I put out for them, they fuss over breakfast until we are all angry and frustrated, and then they noodle out to the car ensuring that we will all be late—again.
- Homework—the kids know they have to get their homework done before they watch TV, but they wait and stall

and ask a hundred questions, give up until finally it's time for bed. Then they are really mad because they didn't get to watch their TV show, I am tired and ready for bed, and we still have another thirty minutes of spelling to get through.

- Bedtime—the kids start stalling just as it's time to start the evening routine. The toothpaste is yucky, they don't want to wear the pajamas, they didn't get to watch their TV show, they want me to lay down with them or read another book, and thirty minutes later we are all fighting as we say goodnight.

- Chores—the kids know I need their help, yet every single time I ask them to do something they give me lip. If I threaten them they will help out, but only that once; if I bribe them, they help out, but only that once. They want me to do everything and still have time to read and play with them.

Part three: Now ask yourself, Why am I so upset about this problem? Write your answers down. You might get answers like:

- The kids won't and can't manage their morning without me, and if I don't intervene we are going to be late for school every day and I will get the hairy eyeball from the ladies in the office.

- The kids won't do their homework without constant supervision and direction, and if they don't do their homework, they will fall behind and won't get into a good college.

- The kids refuse to get ready for bed without my constant nagging and direction, and if I don't go through the routine with them they say I don't love them.

- The kids are lazy and if I don't manipulate them or demand that they help me, they won't do anything ever.

Now freeze and look at your list. You'll start to see where your thinking can get you into trouble. This list will look different for every parent.

Part four: This is where your new thinking begins, and with new thinking comes new responses. If mornings aren't going smoothly and you know you haven't trained your children, then a smooth morning is as simple as stepping back and using your new thinking to guide you in creating morning routines that work for each child. You will need to base each child's routine on her personality and preferences, fostering independence in each one and allowing the kids to try and fail until they develop the resilience to keep forging ahead. (It's not that the kids are mischief-makers, it's that they don't have a system or know what to do or how to do it in the morning.) Notice this isn't about getting your child to do anything differently, it's about pausing and reevaluating your role in the "problem." If you can begin to see exactly where you're willing to change your parenting efforts, then this next section will crack the new thinking experience wide open.

Refer to your list as you begin to work toward change.

Changing Your Thinking Is the Most Difficult Part, but It's Worth It!

After working with thousands of parents, I've realized that it's difficult for them to recognize and admit they must change their perspective and allow for a totally new way of thinking. It's even harder for parents who have been heading in the wrong direction to take ownership for their role in derailing the family dynamic. They often feel as if they've failed, and nothing could be further from the truth.

Changing our thinking and accepting that we may be contributing to the problems we are challenged with means we can now open up to a whole new perspective, one that will change our parenting approach and help us parent from a more intentional, thoughtful, creative, and optimistic place. That's what I call POWER!

I've been doing this for twenty years, and I've heard story after story from discouraged parents who come to talk with me with their heads low and feeling that they have screwed up their kids and messed up their families, and that there are no more options for them. My heart goes out to them. I know how committed they are to their kids and to their roles as parents. I wish I could give them a do-over card, but I can't. What I can do is share a thought I used to encourage myself while I was in the trenches of parenting my own five children.

We are all doing the best we can with the information we have. All we need is new information (thinking) to make a 360-degree change in ourselves and in our families.

Let's do this.

SECTION II

GET OUT THE
DUCT TAPE AND TAKE A
LEAP OF FAITH

At this moment, after all the information covered in section 1, you might be wondering, *How in the world will I integrate all this new thinking into my next sequence of decisions?* The answer is...drumroll, please...DUCT TAPE. This is your chance to shift your focus away from your child's pesky behaviors and habits and focus on what it will take for you to raise an independent, responsible, respectful, and resilient child. You will train yourself to say less, do less, interfere less, and micromanage less, and allow your children to take a more active role in their lives and the life of the family. This will provide opportunities for them to practice new skills, learn from their mistakes, and navigate their own lives whenever possible.

You're going to use duct tape on your mouth, hands, and even your rear end if necessary (literally or figuratively, it's up to you) to refrain from jumping in and taking over. Instead, you will learn to trust that your children can change and will change, and that with new information, you too can change.

When you accept that your role as a parent is to step out rather than step in and fix or interfere or correct, then you will begin to steer your family in the direction you envisioned at the very beginning of parenthood. You'll replace the power struggles, demands, and dysfunction in the family with cooperation, appreciation, and mutual respect. That's it. Duct tape, relationship and training strategies, and faith.

After twenty years, I can honestly say that I continue to use the Duct Tape Method each time the kids and I hit a rough patch. It usually means that I have stopped thinking, started reacting, and I am parenting on autopilot. When this happens, it's a reminder that I need a reality check to ensure that I am actually parenting effectively. After all, kids change as they grow. What seems important one minute is irrelevant the next. The Duct Tape Method is the fastest and most effective way I know of reminding myself what parenting is really about. It's about the long-term relationship I am building with my children and their ability to grow into independent, enthusiastic, engaged adults.

The point of gathering new information, which is possible when we stop talking and start observing, is to help guide our parenting decisions. In the following chapters, I'll outline how a small shift in thinking, along with a more hands-off approach to parenting, can make dramatic, lasting, and astonishing changes in individual family members and in the family as a whole.

What you need to know is that the duct tape will be for *you*, mom and dad. Not the kiddo. So, get ready to tape yourself into new parenting habits. You can actually tape yourself, but a mental visual is just as effective. Please, don't tape yourself into any sticky situations.

6

Duct Tape for the Relationship: Repairing Family Fractures Is a Solution

Love me when I least deserve it, because that is when I really need it.

—Swedish proverb

Who do you feel like cooperating with? Someone who bosses you around or someone who trusts and respects you?

—Vicki Hoefle

Relationship strategies are for parents who want to be in sync with, connected to, tuned in to, and loved by their kids, all while maintaining respect, order, and a level of understanding unique to the family's dynamics. Relationship strategies have the power to solve daily challenges that go along with raising kids, including getting out of the door on time, dealing with sibling squabbles, and having the kids help out without nagging and reminding them. Relationship strategies help parents and kids stay connected during the ups and downs of life in the family zoo and support parents as they learn to let go a bit and trust that their kids are learning to navigate the world in a way that has meaning for them. This is the magic. Once you commit to building a solid relationship with your kids and not micromanaging their behavior, everything shifts.

If that is not reason enough, remember, the next generations are the future leaders of our families, communities, country, and this well-connected planet. If the children of today are to become tomorrow's leaders, doesn't it seem reasonable that they spend time in childhood developing the skills necessary to successfully navigate first their own world and then the world at large? If these same kids are going to make decisions about how I will be treated as an incontinent, toothless ninety-year-old, I want them to have fond memories of me. No kidding. The world is a maze of interconnected relationships that have us either working together or against each other. Our children's introduction to healthy relationships begins at home.

But how exactly does a parent shift from the microcosm of behavior management to the macrocosm of relationship building? Here is one idea I introduce to parents that helps them shift their thinking and open up new possibilities in their parenting.

In every moment, parents are either:

- Interfering with the relationship they have with their child and the child's ability to grow into an independent, capable, responsible, respectful, resilient adult.
- Enhancing their relationship with their child and the child's ability to grow into an independent, capable, responsible, respectful, resilient adult.

Even well-intended parents inadvertently interfere on a regular basis. Many parents *think* that they are enhancing the relationship with their children when they try to drive home

Duct Tape Moment

If you notice you're drilling your kids with questions and thoughts and useless inquiries or criticisms, tape your mouth until you can curb the rapid-fire. Kids don't need guidance and information 24-7. They don't need to walk in the door and be engaged with you and walk you through the minute details of their day. It's a hovering habit that is ineffective at staying connected to your child. You can be quiet and be connected. You can let them get lost in their own worlds—it does not mean you don't care or that your child is slipping away from you.

values and good habits with their micromanagement, corrections, and quick-fix tactics. Here's where the obstacle lies. How can we, the adults, change our parenting approach if we think we are doing what we're supposed to, even if it's not working? Maybe that's why you're still reading this. You know that the relationship matters, but it's the list of "Yeah, buts" and "This isn't workings" that keeps getting in the way. You might understand all of this in theory, but in execution, you come up shy of committing to the relationship.

The First Step

It's time now to shift from your current state of behavior-focused parenting over to a relationship-focused approach to parenting. This move across the hall requires a leap of faith on your part as you put your trust in the idea that letting go and stepping back in certain areas of your parenting will move you to a more satisfying and respectful relationship with your kids (and yes, will still get you out of the house on time without yelling or tears). Accepting that all the interfering strategies actually limit independence and cause more power struggles and discord will also help when it comes time for you to stay quiet, allow life to unravel a bit, and watch quietly while the kids learn to navigate their lives with more confidence and enthusiasm, which is exactly what enhances the relationship and builds independent, capable, responsible, respectful, and resilient kids.

If that sounds inviting, then it's time to let go of what's not working and consciously develop a duct-taped, hands-off, and relationship-focused approach to parenting. It's finally time to toss the interfering junk (ineffective discipline strategies) into the nearest dumpster. In order to do this—to really make a difference in your family—you have to accept that you are in control of what happens next and the changes your family experiences are based on how committed *you* are to changing. What exactly are you going to change? You are going to change two things, your thinking and your approach.

Start Where You Are: What Do You Think about Your Children Today

When I ask parents what their kids do that drives them crazy, they can rattle off an emotionally charged list without hesitation. Remember the list you made way back in chapter 1? "She's stubborn." "He's bossy all the time." "She talks back." "He's messy."

When I ask the same parents to identify the child's strengths, silence falls and eyes shift downward as confusion and embarrassment fills the room. I watch it happen over and over as the mood shifts when parents realize they are more comfortable listing what's wrong than what's right with their children.

Once they begin to rev up with examples and positive descriptions, I see a list that reflects the upside to stubborn (tenacious), bossy (born leader), and strong-willed (knows what he wants).

Here's Where We Start the New Thinking

How would life with your child be different if you reframed your ideas about what constitutes a thinking, engaged, fabulously brilliant, responsible, respectful, resilient child?

What if you don't really want to get rid of all the things that drive you crazy, but rather aim to tweak your child's "negative behaviors" into a strength-filled, useful skill set?

Negative behaviors come from the same place as brilliance. Your kids are just using their unique talents in the wrong direction! It's our job to say, Well, I don't actually want to extinguish that personality trait, I just want to redirect it. Isn't that closer to the real definition of parenting? Helping to guide and direct your children toward the useful side of life as they develop their unique skills, preferences, and talents?

Think about your child. You may have a label or two. Try to look at the label in a more positive light.

- A sassy child is a future entertainer.
- A bossy child is a future leader.
- A noodler is a future stress-management consultant.
- A defiant child is a future civil rights attorney.
- A hyper child is a future teacher.
- A questioning child is a future innovator.

Developing this mental habit helps us naturally shift our focus from trying to "fix" the kids or get them to stop doing something. We automatically see "bad" behaviors as less of a problem and more of a misfired character trait. We start to care less about what others say because we know we're working on developing a better outlet for that bossiness or back talk.

Parenting is not about raising kids who make us look good in front of our friends, it's about preparing kids for their future and teaching them how to take what they have and apply it in useful, respectful, and powerful ways to influence the world around them. How many of us were labeled bossy, sassy, or lazy when we were young? It's what you do with it that matters, right?

To do this right now, you have to forget about every other child in the world, drop all your expectations, and forget all the mistakes you've made. Then you have to commit to:

- **Meeting your child where she is today** (bossy) and allowing her to grow and change over the course of eighteen years with your guidance (into a leader).
- **Worrying less about what everyone else thinks** about your child's behavior (bossy) and accepting that he is doing the best he can in any given moment (he's five, cut him some slack).
- **Ignoring the occasional "hairy eyeball"** encountered in the checkout line (she's bossing you again), because you know that you are raising a thinking child and thinking children can be messy at times. (Hey, it's not personal, she's practicing for when she's CEO, right?)
- **Setting aside your concerns about your child's future "potential"** (bossy means no friends) and focusing more on what he's learning about himself and the world with each new encounter ("Hmmm, the kids on

the playground don't seem all that thrilled with my bossy nature").

- **Recognizing that your child will create the life that supports who she is**, what she cares about, and the values she holds sacred. (I like being the boss of my life and allowing others to be the boss of their lives.)

Now that your mind is primed, you are ready to respond differently, to let go a bit in order to focus on and strengthen the relationship you have with your children. After all, if we want to be powerful influences in our children's lives, and that includes the teen years, then we have to be in communication with them. And if we are micromanaging, lecturing, interfering, and demanding, it's likely we will hear the slam of a bedroom door before we hear an invitation to sit on the edge of the bed and share the day.

Fifteen Relationship Strategies

The following fifteen relationship strategies are designed to help you parent when you aren't at critical mass. They will help you shift your parenting approach from a reactive to a proactive, intentional, thoughtful, and hands-off approach that has you handing more and more responsibility over to your children, providing the necessary training to ensure their success in a way that instills confidence in both you and the children.

You will use these strategies as inspiration when you're out there in the trenches, those times when you want to step in but you decide to wait it out, or when you want to save your child but you opt to let the lesson run its course. This list, paired with mental duct tape (which we'll get to next) and the courage to have faith, is all you will need to change course and find success that you and your children will notice and enjoy.

1. Mistakes are opportunities to learn. We've all heard this before. What you might not be hearing is the subconscious tendency to finish that sentence with, "as long as those mistakes don't disrupt my life, embarrass me in public, or have the coach giving me the hairy eyeball. If they do, I'm stepping in and tinkering with the opportunity."

Mistakes are arguably the easiest and most efficient way for kids to learn to cooperate, take personal responsibility, practice time management, develop organizational skills, become resilient, and develop the mental muscle that will come in handy as their lives become more challenging and difficult in the years to come. Parents interfere with the most efficient and effective relationship strategy on the market—mistakes—because of the fear of being judged. I wanted to print up funny little kid t-shirts years ago that said, "Thinking kids are messy. Obviously, I'm a genius."

Kidding aside, we have to allow for mountains of mistakes and pause before we intervene, not to solve, but to find out what the child is learning from the experience. Once we know where the child is, we can put in place a plan to build on the experience.

Here is a note I received from a parent on the subject of mistakes:

Mistakes, mistakes, and more mistakes. I thought I was a parent who really embraced the whole "mistakes are opportunities to learn" approach. But it didn't take me more than a few days to realize that every time my kids came even close to making a mistake I was there to redirect them. Of course, in my mind I was thinking, "now that I have told them what will happen if they make that choice, they can avoid making the mistake and learn the lesson." Disaster averted, right? Wrong. The opposite happened, of course. They were doomed to make the same mistake over and over again because I kept interfering. I had no idea how focused I was on staying away from mistakes. Fast-forward three months and I can't tell you the difference between where we were and where we are now as a family. My new motto? Bring on the mistakes, kids, life is practice.

2. Take time to train the kids to participate in running the house. This is so crucial to a healthy relationship that I have an entire chapter dedicated to making it happen. In chapter 8 I walk you through a system I have been using for twenty years that will have you throwing down your apron and hitting snooze while your kids get themselves out of bed and jam through their morning routine. They'll be cleaning their messes and looking out for themselves. You'll finally be able to walk away or leave the room without hovering, micromanaging, or even caring how spotless the floors are because you know your kids will have plenty of time to practice and improve. Besides having a clean and tidy house, you are raising kids who are independent, organized, helpful, and considerate and who understand that work comes before play. How cool is that?

3. Focus on your child's strengths and innate talents. As nice as we find the idea of living with a child who is compliant and who obeys, remains quiet, and does as we ask, most parents I talk with would rather raise a thinking, engaged, industrious, curious child who participates in life. Focusing on a child's strengths and innate talents does several things. First, it's really hard for a child to fight with a parent who keeps pointing out all his strengths and assets. Second, we know that kids whose strengths are pointed out continue to develop them and, as that happens, some of the peskier behaviors show up less and less. And finally, the message the child hears from the parent is, What you *do* when you are frustrated (scream) is not who you are. Who you *are* is determined in the quiet moments when you feel most relaxed, assured, and confident.

Maggie shared the following with me over coffee:

I thought I was a parent who could rattle off her child's strengths, but when you challenged me to write down twenty strengths my child had, I was hard pressed to come up with even six legitimate ones. I spent a few weeks observing my kids and I realized that I overlook so many of their strengths because they aren't completely developed. The minute I changed my focus and began to blow on those small embers, they caught fire, and now I can rattle off thirty of my kids' strengths without missing a beat. The change in the relation-ship—well, how would you feel being in a relationship with someone who just kept telling you how amazing you were and shining a light on all the things that make you an incredible human being?

4. Create routines (it's easier than you think). As a family, identify a time of day that has been particularly rough (morning can generally be counted on as one of the most chal-lenging times in any family) and agree to create a routine that supports each member individually and the family as a whole.

- Identify the goal: our goal is to be out of the house by 7:15 A.M. on four out of five mornings a week with no one in tears and no one yelling.
- Ask family members to describe what their perfect morning would look like. This will provide valuable information (information that is bound to surprise you in the most wonderful ways).

- Write down similarities in stories and look for common threads you can build on (two of the kids like to get up twenty minutes before the bus arrives, you and your middle child need ninety minutes to feel prepared).
- Work out the details that support each of your preferences. You don't all have to do the morning in exactly the same way. Those who like to eat on the run can now find five options in the lower drawer. Those who like to have a leisurely breakfast can find five options in the top drawer. It's easy if you are willing to get creative.
- Agree to practice and allow for things to go wrong before you find just the right routine. Practice and improvement is what we are going for here. Remember, you want to be shown the same latitude and flexibility in your life, so extend it to your kids as they learn to identify and implement daily routines.
- Allow the kids to learn by making mistakes like sleeping through the alarm clock, forgetting a backpack, or not leaving time to eat breakfast. This is how kids learn. They do not learn because you are nagging, reminding, lecturing, or bribing them to get themselves moving in the morning. If they did learn that way, you'd already be enjoying a breezy stroll out the front door.

Following is a story from my own life that illustrates the power of routines:

When my youngest daughter was in the second grade, home-work became an issue. Her dad is a teacher by profession and I come from a long line of teachers, so doing well in school is important to us. She began to throw quiet, determined, stand-offish temper tantrums. In other words, she just plain refused to do the homework. Almost every night she was in tears and her dad and I were lecturing, nagging, micromanaging, scolding, threatening, or bribing her to do her homework. She flat out refused. We would go to bed feeling like complete heels.

To make it worse, I am a professional parent educator and my darn second grader had me completely stumped. Finally, after several conversations with my husband, it clicked. The next morning at breakfast, I asked her the magic question.

"K, in a perfect world, on a perfect day, how would you take care of your homework?" She did not hesitate. She had been waiting for us to listen to her.

"I would get up at 4:30 A.M. and do it. I can't do it at night. My brain just won't do it."

"Okay, I said. How about for the next week, you do your homework whenever you like. Your dad and I will not get in your way. Here is the thing though, we have to leave the house at 7:15 A.M. No exceptions. Can you do that?"

She thought for maybe ten seconds and then said, "YES."

We were ready for this to flop (because I'll admit, like most parents, I believed homework was really a nighttime thing, even though everyone was usually wiped out when it came time to get it done, and I had never thought of it otherwise). Still, we went into it with the hope that this might actually work.

The very next morning, my husband got up at his usual 5:15 A.M. and headed out to the kitchen. And who did he find at the kitchen table with a cup of tea and her math book opened up? You guessed it, our second grader.

This second grader is now in college and she has been doing her homework at 4:30 in the morning ever since this lesson unfolded. In fact, she has now established an early bird group with other students who have tendencies like hers, but who didn't tap into them because their parents fought with them about the appropriate time for doing homework. You can see this one piece of information served our daughter well throughout her educational experience and it continues to serve her. Imagine the fighting and discord that would have been created had we refused to allow her to create a routine that worked for her.

As parents, there are countless little battles that we fight simply because we haven't stopped to ask our kids if there's another way and if they'd be willing to try it that way. Once we look around, we find almost everything has a variety of possibilities. We just have to keep it moving and bend when our kids think of something we never dreamed of. Like the kid I know who, at about first grade, decided to get dressed at night (for efficiency's sake) and hop up, brush his teeth, and bolt out the door in the morning. Off he went through fifth grade, in those jeans he didn't mind sleeping in every night. Who'd have thought?

5. Include kids in the decision-making process. Yes, I know this sounds scary. You're probably hesitant to hand over the reins. But think about it this way: your kids are already involved in the decision-making process. Basically, you make all the decisions and they squash them. So, you might as well bring them into the discussion and work toward training them to actually *help* the family instead of interrupting the flow.

If your kids keep rebelling and you keep nagging them to do a chore, why not ask them how they think it should be done. You never know! Maybe they think trash night is inconvenient because after dinner they're warm and cozy inside. But in the morning, they've already got shoes on, so it would be better to do it then, which sounds agreeable. (And—as a bonus—they're more likely to show up when they've had a part in creating the flow of the family schedule.)

You don't have to include them in every decision, but my experience with kids shows that the more involved they are, the more investment they have in maintaining the health and well-being of the family. Start small, show some faith, and watch as your kids become expert decision makers. That's a skill that might pay off when they leave home at eighteen.

Arthur, a father of three, shared this in a group I was facilitating for recently single parents:

> *It doesn't seem like such a big thing when they are young. They can help make decisions about family time and meals and where they will keep their stuff. But here is the thing. Because we invited the kids into the process when they were young, it spilled out into the other areas of their life. They became skillful decision makers when it came to managing their money, their time, their friendships, and their schoolwork. Each time they stepped up and took ownership of their decisions, we witnessed their confidence grow and their decision-making skills improve.*

6. Hold regular family meetings. ATTENTION: "Family meetings" are *not* held in response to problems. They are proactive communication meetings. They are *not* designed for kids to sit at the table as the parents list off all the ways the kids are screwing up and how the kids must change in order for the family to function properly. (Seriously, don't even waste your time if this is how you think the meetings should be run! You will get the FAMILY MEETING FAIL experience and it won't put anyone in a better place.)

Family meeting basics:

- Commit to one evening a week and stick to it.
- Put fifteen to twenty minutes on the timer.

- Everyone is invited, no one is required to attend.
- Have each family member share something they appreciate about every other member of the family. If you want
  to raise kids who are kind to each other and show appreciation for you, this is where it starts.
- Use the time to schedule activities, special times, school
  events, etc.
- Hand out allowances at the end (general guide = $1/
  year of age, $5 for a five-year-old). If you want to avoid
  fighting every time you enter a store and teach your kids
  how to manage their money, pass the cash and watch the
  magic unfold.
- Repeat each week. (Note: because family meetings are
  sequential and roles build over time, visit our website
  www.parentingontrack.com for additional information.)
- Start here. You'll see magic.

7. Create a family roadmap. I've been asking parents for
more than fifteen years if they have a "parenting roadmap"
(parenting is a journey, after all) to guide them through the
task of raising an infant into adulthood. I ask them if they have
a map for where they are today (I scream at my kids and my
kids scream back), where they want to be in a week (one less
day of screaming on both our parts), where they want to be
in six months (no screaming by anyone in the family), where
they want to be when their child turns eighteen (mutually
respectful conversation), and a plan for how they are going
to get there? Right. No one has one. The hours that parents
spend on picking out names and colors for the baby's room is
disproportionate to how many hours they spend creating an
intentional, thoughtful, and reasonable plan for raising their
kids. In chapter 10 I will show you how to create a roadmap for
you and your family.

8. Be a role model. Actually, you already are a role model. What I mean is, if you expect your child to act like a rational, thoughtful, respectful, patient human being after she has been trying to zip her coat up for ten minutes, she will have had to see her parent model rational, thoughtful, respectful, patient behavior in times of frustration, stress, disappointment, and so on after a particularly lousy day at the office.

Parents have no right to expect more from their children than they expect from themselves. When a parent has personal permission to throw temper tantrums, lash out, yell, belittle, or disrespect, it is reasonable to extend that same courtesy to the children. I have a little secret to share—your children are not picking up their pesky behaviors and attitudes from the other children in class, or from video games, television, music, or the "naughty" cousin they see on holidays. They are mimicking you.

Use this thinking the next time you find yourself yelling or about to lash out at your child for being mean or talking rudely to a sibling. Are you, in fact, sounding the exact same way? Freeze, and think before you act. Role modeling is happening 24/7, so if you just change your tone, delivery, and response to model what you want to see from your kids, you'll find you will get the same from them.

9. Start an appreciation board. When my daughter was fifteen years old, she came home one day in a particularly foul mood. She marched past the appreciation board and up to her room. Everyone in the family gave one another knowing looks. It could prove to be an exceptionally long night. My oldest son walked over to the appreciation board and wrote something on it about his older sister. Her other three siblings followed suit and so did her dad and I. When she next graced us with her presence, I walked her over to the board and asked her if she would read aloud all the appreciations written down that applied to her.

"I appreciate H for finding the courage last week to stay away from a party where there would be booze and drugs."

"I appreciate H for helping me do my hair yesterday, even though it made her have to put hers in a sloppy bun."

"I appreciate H for letting me come sit on her bed at night when I can't sleep and talk to me until I can fall asleep— and sometimes she lets me sleep with her."

There were nine of those messages on the board. When she came to number five, she turned around, looked at all of us, and declared,

"Do you know how hard it is to be a teenager in this house?"

And then she smiled, thanked all of us, and said she was feeling much better and that she must be the luckiest sister in the world. It's easy to turn a potentially negative situation into a positive one if you don't try to talk your kid out of or solve whatever it is that is upsetting her. Just be willing to extend to your teenager the same courtesies you would extend to a friend who was having a crummy day. It's not so easy if you think a kid who is rude has to be punished, controlled, and lectured. I know that's the tricky part; once our kids are rude, we think that gives us license to be.

10. Become your child's mentor not corrector. You can decide to wear any parenting hat you want. There are no fast and hard rules. Who wants to be in relationship with a constant corrector? Not me, and I bet you don't either. Why do we even entertain the notion that our kids will find any pleasure from being corrected each time they attempt to make a choice? Honor their feelings (no matter what they are) when they try something new (which they don't do to perfection the first thirty-six times). Mentoring allows us to look for ways to inspire, guide, teach, train, and support our kids as they grow and learn. Try putting on this new and powerful hat and watch the response you start to see in your kids.

11. Focus on effort, improvement, and progress and forget all about perfection. Unless you yourself have arrived at a state of perfection—stash it. Would you want me walking into your homes and making judgments about your commitment to parenting based on how "perfectly" you followed a set of instructions with outcomes that included perfectly behaved kids? Of course you wouldn't. Focus on the progress. Accept that people are doing the best they can. Verbalize the improvement and growth in your kids and you are bound to get more of it.

This is from Nancy, a self-proclaimed reformed perfectionist:

I was one of those moms who took pride in saying I was a perfectionist until I saw what the impact was on the kids. I had created a home where my kids were afraid to try anything new because I refused to celebrate with them until they achieved— yup—perfection. There wasn't much celebrating going on in my house. They were also becoming master criticizers and were avoiding trying new things. I can't believe it took me so long to see this. Today, we celebrate our lives. We celebrate the small successes and the improvement we are making. The atmosphere in the house is completely different. We are all more relaxed and excited about what life has to offer and about supporting each other.

12. Ignore it, and by *it*, I mean everything (unless it's morally or physically dangerous). Why do I consider this a relationship strategy? Because, in truth, if we could just shut our mouths (duct tape is really good for this) and allow a stressful moment to pass with no snarky comment or a follow-up dig, it will, in fact, go away on its own. Yes, even the squabble over the remote or the lost toy meltdown will lift. If you can stay out of it, I guarantee the lifespan of the situation will be reduced and diminished. If it keeps happening, try ignoring it longer, because the kids might really just be trying to engage you with their antics and get you to go back to your old ways! If the behavior continues and seems to escalate, then you know it's a bigger relationship problem, and will take some of these other relationship strategies to mend. But if you focus on mending the relationship, the behavior will diminish as the relationship is rejuvenated.

Ignoring doesn't mean that you won't address a situation, but doing it when everyone is heated never ends well. Give yourself time to cool down, to observe what's really going on, and to give the situation a chance to end on its own, and then find a reasonable time to talk about the bigger issue.

13. Encourage! Encourage! Encourage! Dr. Rudolf Dreikurs said, "Encouragement is more important than any other aspect of child-raising. It is so important that the lack of it can be considered the basic cause for misbehavior. A misbehaving child *is* a discouraged child."

Encouragement is an observation. To encourage, you notice: *you are hurt, you are angry, you tied your shoe, you got an A, or you flunked the test.* There is no judgment attached to the observation. It is a way to open up a conversation and allow children to share their experience and their feelings with someone they trust.

Encouragement is acknowledging. To encourage, you tell someone: *your help made the job easier, your sense of humor had me giggling instead of crying,* or *you helped your brother even though you wanted to watch your show.* To acknowledge how someone made a difference in a situation or in your day or in your life sends the message to the person that she is valuable and that you appreciate who she is.

Encouragement focuses on effort and improvement, and it can be given anytime. Encouragement sounds like: *you are tying your shoe faster than you were last week, you are passing the ball more on the field, or you are walking away more often.* As a child, knowing that someone is noticing the fact that you are getting better at difficult tasks inspires you to keep going. For many parents, to encourage just requires leaving the *and I'm so proud of you* off the end of the statement.

Encouragement is meant to inspire children to take risks, make choices, and assume responsibility for those choices and actions.

Encouragement teaches kids to rely on themselves for self-evaluation instead of looking for outside validation, which builds healthy, strong, fortified self-esteem and helps kids feel satisfied and grounded in their own lives.

Encouragement instills an attitude of resiliency, aware-ness, kindness, empathy, forgiveness, and patience.

Encouragement focuses on the process, not on the end result.

Here's an example. Let's say your seven-year-old child wants to carry the twenty dollars he's been saving in his wallet and you say, "Okay, sure, how do you think you want to take care of the wallet?" And he gives a good response but you're not convinced he'll be able to keep track of the wallet. He wants to carry it because he feels quite grown up opening and closing that thing at every counter, showing off the bills.

You sit by (as hard as it is) and watch as he, sure enough, accidentally loses the wallet at the movies. Here's where you *could* (but you don't) come in and say, "I told you so" as he's crying and feeling the pain of this. He just learned the value of taking care of the money. It'll only take once. This is the moment to say, "I can see how upset losing the wallet is to you. What could you do differently next time?" With a little support and a bit of brainstorming, an upset child suddenly shifts into problem-solving master and a new confidence is established.

Encouragement is the confirmation that those natural lessons are necessary and that it's okay when things don't go according to the plan. What's important is the knowledge that you can overcome any obstacle, solve any problem, and recover from any situation. When you create an encouraging environment for your children, two things happen right away. The first is a decrease in pesky, negative behaviors and the second is a more resilient, flexible, and relaxed child. That sounds like a winning combination to me.

14. Get curious. Ask questions and look for clues your child gives you about the ways she interprets the world around her. Stop assuming you know what is happening in your child's mind. I tell parents in all of my classes that if they can remember this image, quoted from psychotherapist Alfred Adler, they will go a long way to fortifying a solid relationship with the kids: "*Hear with their ears, see with their eyes, and feel with their heart.*"

Each night, your children go to bed having made the most of their day. They have gathered information, analyzed situations, and made course corrections. When they wake up in the morning and walk into the kitchen, you are greeting entirely new people. Get to know *these* people again. Parents have a tendency to summarize their kids and create labels for them and forget that the kids are in the process of growing and changing every single day. They also tend to treat their nine-year-olds as if they are still three. Being curious about your kids keeps you up to date with who they are becoming, and you are in a better position to support their budding independence, which ultimately leads to fewer power struggles.

15. Show faith. Trust that these strategies will work. Trust that your children are capable of more than you imagine and that they will learn through your guidance and the natural consequences the world will provide. Have faith in yourself, your children, and the world at large, and life with kids will become a source of joy, satisfaction, and deep connection. In chapters 11, 12, and 13 I share stories from kids and families to illustrate just how powerful a little faith can be in bringing out the best in each of us.

Incorporating even one of these strategies into your daily life with kids will make a difference in the quality of the relationship you have with them. Start slow and allow yourself time to make mistakes as well as experience progress and improvement. Have fun and give the strategies time to work. If you need a little help in developing patience, go ahead, grab the duct tape.

7

Duct Tape for the Mouth: Keeping Your Mind Open and Your Mouth Closed Is a Solution

Wise men, when in doubt whether to speak or to keep quiet, give themselves the benefit of the doubt, and remain silent.

—Napoleon Hill

Parenting wisdom comes when you shut your mouth, open your ears, and observe with your eyes. Until then, it's all guessing games.

—Vicki Hoefle

In section 1, I dissected all the ways parents end up over-involved, over-reactive, and over-directive. Out of a need to keep things moving with as little friction as possible, parents become the feeders of the "weeds" and the "doers of too much." You've likely been here—your two-year-old is noodling and you begin to coax her along. Your three-year-old won't get dressed, even though he can, so you start nagging. Your four-year-old won't stay at the table and eat her breakfast, so you start lecturing and bribing her. Your five-year-old refuses to brush his teeth unless you remind him a dozen times before he leaves for school. Your six-year-old leaves his stuff scattered around the house and you make it your job to nag, remind, lecture, count, and then do it yourself, in order to make it to work on time. Your seven-year-old refuses to get up with his alarm clock, so you wake him up every morning even though you swear you won't do it again the following day. Your eight- and six-year-olds tease and fight, and you are counting, time-outing, and punishing to get them to stop.

In the process of micromanaging your kids' lives, you have also created a set of assumptions about what would happen if you *stopped* your hands-on, over-involved, fix-it style of parenting. And those assumptions are generally packed with fear about how out of control your kids, your family, and your life would be if you stopped doing what you are currently doing to maintain order.

And once a set of assumptions has been created, parents begin using them to make the majority of their parenting decisions (including choosing *not* to do things differently), and those decisions create the environment in your home and the dynamic between you and your kids. Enter, interfering discipline strategies, Band-Aid tactics, and a cycle of discord that can last for years! It's these assumptions that account for a parent's resistance to letting go and making the changes necessary to bring a little balance, order, and fun back to parenting.

Parents' Assumptions Are Based on Existing Information (Pssst, It's Time to Get New Information)

If you've spent more than two or three years stepping in and helping out and directing and reminding, it's understandable that you might have developed a set of assumptions that include: without my constant involvement my kids will fall apart, fight incessantly, leave their stuff all over the house, treat us with disregard, break every rule, and turn into little beasts who take over the house.

With this set of assumptions driving our parenting decisions and supporting a hands-on, micromanaging approach, there is no room for the kids to do anything but take a back-seat attitude to life.

Look around, today more than ever, kids are disconnected from their everyday lives and don't seem to be paying much attention to what's happening around them. Honestly, though, why would they? Parents are so proficient at managing and directing them that the kids aren't required to pay attention and plug into their own lives. These kids don't have to worry about getting up with an alarm clock because mom comes in six times every morning to ensure they are up. These kids don't have to worry about weather-appropriate clothes, because mom and dad tell them what is acceptable to wear and

Duct Tape Moment

Use the sticky stuff to cover the mirror you've been looking in. There is nothing that says you have to look perfect, be perfect, and keep your family in perfect order to be a good mother. Your kids' behaviors are not a walking reflection on whether or not you are good parents. Kids' behaviors are based on their drive to find themselves, and to fit in and be part of something. If they screw up, it certainly doesn't mean you've been neglecting your job as a mother or father. Stop and think, will any of this matter in twenty minutes? Two days? Two weeks? The answer is most often no, so it's fine to let things go.

what isn't. These kids don't have to manage their time, because their parents have every minute of the day calculated and the child merely goes from one task to the other with prompts from mom and dad. These kids aren't required to problem solve, because mom and dad step in whenever there is any disruption in the house. Kids don't help around the house until mom or dad starts in with lecturing and threatening.

If we want to raise thinking kids with the mental muscle to navigate an ever-changing world, then we have to provide them with daily opportunities to learn to construct a meaningful and satisfying life and teach them the skills necessary to manage that life. What better place for children to practice than in their own home with the guidance of loving and wise parents?

But unfortunately, even parents who want to raise thinking kids are trapped by faulty assumptions and generalized fears that make it difficult to take a hands-off approach to parenting. Until those assumptions are put under the spotlight and flushed out with accurate information, nothing is going to change for long. It takes a serious jolt for parents to rethink and reframe their assumptions, but this jolt allows them to become masters of a more hands-off (for the good of the child) approach to parenting.

Here's a list of actions based on existing information and the assumptions that they reveal:

Existing Action	Assumption
Mom puts clothing out for the child.	The child will not get up and get dressed appropriately for school without my help.
Dad pours cereal every morning.	The child will make a mess, and won't pick a healthy breakfast.

Existing Action	Assumption
Mom packs the backpack before school.	The children will go to school unprepared.
Dad controls child's allowance spending, decides what is appropriate.	The kid will buy candy bars all day long, and blow his money on nonsense.
Mom and dad lecture, call teachers to explain late assignments.	The child will get into the habit of turning papers in late, will do poorly in school, and won't get into a good college.
Mom constantly corrects rude, lazy, or "improper" behavior.	Kids will become rude, lazy, or get into bad habits.

It's clear that in most cases a child would be physically and intellectually capable of handling every task or making every choice detailed here. This chart, or the version you create for yourself, will expose your own faulty assumptions. When it does, you will be in a position to replace them with facts that will guide your parenting decisions in the future!

Claire's Thinking Is Based on What If Instead of What Is

"I will admit it," Claire said. "I nag, remind, lecture, count, micromanage, threaten, bribe, and save my kids, and I know now that all of those so-called strategies are interfering in the relationship I have with my kids and their chance at becoming independent, self-sufficient, and resilient. See, I have been listening. But I am telling you right now, Vicki, that if I don't do all of those things, my kids will not do one thing they are supposed to do in the morning or any other time of day."

"How do you know that?" I asked.

"Because, I know my kids," Claire answered.

"Tell me what you think they will do," I said.

"I think they will stay in bed all day, sleep through their alarms, get up when they feel like it, come downstairs and blame me because I didn't wake them up, sit at the counter and demand I feed them, then start to cry because they don't know how to get dressed without help, and then, finally, sit on the couch and ask *me* to turn the television on for them so they can watch a show."

"You really don't believe they will do anything without your assistance?"

"Well, they might try to do a few things, but they will either leave a mess or they will fight with each other, or they will just give up, or they will eat a candy bar for breakfast. It will be a disaster."

"And you know all of this will happen—how? Have you ever left them alone in the morning?"

"No. Never. I just told you, I can't."

"Okay, so what you are telling me is that you *think* you know what your kids will do if you aren't nagging, reminding, lecturing, and so on, but that you don't really know for a fact what will happen because you've never stepped back and watched."

"Yes."

"And is there an age at which your children will suddenly be able to do all these things on their own, perfectly, or will you continue to nag, remind, and lecture until they leave home at eighteen?"

Silence.

"Would you like to find out what will really happen if you take a more hands-off approach to your parenting and give up all those Band-Aid tactics and ineffective discipline strategies you're using now? Do you really want to know what will happen when you stop feeding the weeds and give the kids a chance to plug back into life?"

"Yes!"

My Kids Won't Do Anything on Their Own (Or Will They? It's Time to Find Out)

Even when parents are 100 percent committed to shifting to a relationship-focused, hands-off approach to parenting, replacing the assumptions with facts is tough. They have to be willing to set aside nagging, reminding, interfering, micro-managing (refer to the list in chapter 1), and their other assortment of Band-Aid tactics for a few days to gather accurate information about what's really going on under their roofs. I developed the Do Nothing, Say Nothing Exercise, which uses, yes, duct tape (on you, not your kid), for just this purpose.

This one exercise consistently, for more than twenty years, has revealed to parents what their kids are really capable of when they step back and give the kids some space and a chance to play a more active role in their own lives. By the time they finish, everything they thought they knew about themselves, their kids, and their family is turned upside down. When that happens, we can begin working together to create the family of their dreams. Nothing is as powerful and eye opening as this one simple exercise. So be ready, because things are about to change!

EXERCISE: DO NOTHING, SAY NOTHING: THE FIVE-DAY DUCT TAPE CHALLENGE

For the next five days, I challenge you to throw your assumptions out the door along with the reminding, nagging, lecturing, and any other Band-Aid tactics you may be using. Grab the duct tape for your mouths and actually observe what happens when you stop talking, start watching, and leave your kids alone long enough for them to show you how capable they are. As Doug Larson says: Wisdom is the reward you get for a lifetime of listening when you'd have preferred to talk.

Because I never ask my students to do anything I haven't done myself, I share my own experience the first time I did this exercise and elicited the help of duct tape.

I thought I could be trusted to stay quiet and watch my kids for a week, but I wasn't willing to bet the bank on it. So I put little strips of duct tape along my kitchen counter in case I needed help staying quiet. Although I *promised* that I would keep my mouth shut for the day and simply observe my kids in action, my mouth was so accustomed to yapping without restraint that I was grabbing for the duct tape after only five minutes in the room with the kids. Each time I was tempted to prompt my kids, I grabbed a piece of duct tape and slapped it over my lips. The first few times I ripped the duct tape off, I found that it not only kept me from interfering with the kids, but it also removed my facial hair above my lip—an added bonus, I thought. Unfortunately, by day two when I took the tape off it was ripping the skin off my lip, which hurt—a lot— and it was then that I realized just how much free rein I was giving myself in terms of directing my kids' lives. I got serious then, and although I left the duct tape on the counter as a reminder, I found the discipline to keep quiet.

Now, before you blow a gasket and start yelling that I have *no* idea how awful things will be in your home if you try this, let me first say that I have been using this same exercise for twenty years because it works, and I have heard all the horror stories and all the stories of success. I've seen the pictures and read the notes kids send in with their parents that chastise me for suggesting to their mom and dad that they stop waiting on their kids. Never once, in all these years, has anything bad ever happened. The fact that parents are genuinely upset and concerned about this exercise says a lot about the overall atmosphere in their homes.

Common Sense or Literal Interpretation?

Whenever I introduce this exercise, I'm certain to hear a concern that sounds something like this:

"I'm struggling here. I am a very literal person. Are you saying I have to Do Nothing and Say Nothing while my kids run wild?"

"No." I explain. "That's not what I am saying. I'm saying to parent without using any of those old interfering, micromanaging, Band-Aid tactics you normally use and to watch and document what happens when you do that. You may use any other parenting strategies you have in your arsenal, including common sense."

Then I get a look of "aha." I wait and watch as they run this statement through their minds, searching and cataloging any parenting strategies they have stored away that do not fall into the category of interfering. Sometimes they light up with the creative challenge; other times, I hear a sigh. Either way, parents realize that the one thing they cannot do is use the strategies that are so clearly not working.

To offer a bit of encouragement to a large group of stunned parents, one mom offered her insight after having done the exercise the year before:

Common sense can be a strategy in and of itself to get you through the exercise. My five-year-old daughter left the food out after helping me make her smoothie this morning. I opened my mouth to say something. Shut it again. Opened it again. Shut it again. I must've looked like a fish on a hook that morning, all the while telling myself, It's only food. It's only money. I can go buy more if it goes bad.

Finally, I realized that my daughter didn't know that she was supposed to put the things away since I got them out for her. *So, I opened my mouth again and said,* "Honey, when we make your breakfast together, I'm putting you in charge of putting things away." "Oh," *she said, and immediately put all of the food back in the fridge, even the stuff that usually goes on the top shelf. She found a place for the fruits, yogurt, and the milk on another shelf that was within her reach. And, despite its precarious and questionable position, I did not go in and move the milk carton that was certain to crash and make a mess all over my floor (even though* I really wanted to say, "Honey, the milk carton looks like it's going to spill!" I didn't). *If it fell, well, she was in charge and she'd see that wasn't a good location. I had to just bite my tongue. Guess what? The milk carton survived and if it had fallen, it would have only been spilled milk!*

What do I know now that I didn't know before? I know my child will help if I take the time to teach her. I know that I use my assumptions to make a quick parenting decision and that almost always causes trouble down the line, and I learned that it is really hard to throw all those awful gimmicks out the window when you realize you don't know what else to do. This was an eye-opening five days, to say the least.

Now, It's Your Turn

Set yourself up for success. Try these tips for "smooth" chaos:

1. Take some time to really note the interfering strategies you're using, what you are "doing for" your kids, and what your assumptions are. Have your list of interfering or Band-Aid tactics nearby so you can refer to the list when you really feel the need to jump in and do damage control.

2. Decide how many days you will engage in this exercise (I recommend five; any fewer and the kids can hold out until you jump back to your old ways.)

3. Make a list of your worst-case scenarios and specific fears (similar to assumptions, but this time to help you accept what might happen—write them in an affirmative way, so that you can accept truth!) Print it and hang it on your fridge or on your mirror.

It could read like this:

- Yes, the house will be messy. But we will live.
- Yes, the laundry may pile up everywhere, but this is good information.
- No, you do not need to wake the kids up, even if they sleep through the alarm.
- Just because the kids might forget their homework, it doesn't mean you're not doing your job as a parent.
- The five days will end and I will have new information that gets my family back on track and moving in a more positive and productive direction.

4. Sit the kids down and tell them the following. Keep it matter of fact; you're not judging or "grading them," you're just interested in stopping your nagging and so on: "We don't like the fact that we are nagging, reminding, lecturing (whatever it is you do on a regular basis with your kids) you every day and we want to stop doing it. That means that starting tomorrow, we are going to stay quiet and watch what happens if we aren't telling you what to do."

Make a verbal list of the hang-ups and worst-case scenarios together: What will the day look like? What happens in the morning? (Go through the day very quickly just to get a feel for where the kids might actually require your assistance, but refrain from giving them last-minute notes on what to do.) Affirm with them the same thoughts:

> *Now, things could be really messy. You might be late for school and that's okay. You might go to school without your lunch, and that's okay. You might forget a coat or your homework or your backpack and that's okay. The house might be really messy and we might run out of dishes and that's okay. Or, things might go great. Without us in your way, maybe you will show us that we were worried for nothing. That you can get up on your own and get dressed and make breakfast and clean up and remember your stuff. Whatever happens is fine. This is a time for us to step back and to watch what you can do all on your own without any help from us. At the end of the five days, we are going to talk about how we can make our family work better for everyone.*

5. Get your duct tape out and put it where you can access it easily.

6. Understand that things will be messy, really messy, and that your kids could be angry, frustrated, confused, elated, or liberated. Use the stories in this chapter to help get through the tough spots. Also, check out these blogs from parents who have completed my parenting program:

flockmother.wordpress.com
parentingontracktales.wordpress.com

7. If you mess up and find yourself feeding the weeds, using Band-Aid tactics, or making assumptions, take a deep breath and start again.

8. At the end of the five days you will have information that will change the way you parent and the way you view your kids. And remember, keep track of the information and write notes. Blog about your experience. Take pictures. Make a chart in your office—keep quiet yet be active in cataloging your mental reflections.

PLEASE NOTE: I am *not* suggesting that you stop parenting. All I am suggesting is that you stop using anything that interferes with the relationship you have with your children and their ability to become independent, responsible, respectful, and resilient people.

If the kids are doing something that's physically or morally dangerous, step in. If the kids are very young, simply watch your tendency to jump in, maneuver, help, or direct the child.

Use your own common sense.

Let's Get Real about Your Assumptions and Your Realities

Here is a table that will make it easier for you to document what's really going on in your homes so that you can:

- Calm your fears
- Gather information for future use
- Refer to it as needed

The first two blocks are filled in as examples; use the rest of the blocks to chart your own set of actions, assumptions, and results.

Your Existing Action	Assumption	What Happened? (To be filled in after the Five-Day Challenge)	Reality (To be reflected upon after the Five-Day Challenge)
I pack all the lunches (for kids ages seven and nine).	The kids will go to school hungry, starve, and freak out at me for not making lunch.	They got mad at me, but I kept quiet (it lasted like two minutes!); they forgot their lunches, borrowed $ twice, made lunch on Friday.	They survived, learned what it's like without lunch, and can make lunches—they were doing okay by day five; they can do lunches! (We'll work on training.)
I do all the dishes, even though I ask for help.	The dish pile will continue to grow and we'll have no dishes, the kitchen will get messy, and nobody will notice except me.	The kids noticed and asked me to wash dishes; I kept my mouth shut; they eventually grabbed a bowl and spoon, rinsed and used them. They got by but lacked any interest in doing the whole load.	They were willing to wash one or two bowls as needed; they noticed how many dishes piled up; they didn't really initiate washing the entire load—that's something to train them on.

Excerpts from the Do Nothing, Say Nothing Diaries

Below are true stories from real parents who completed the Do Nothing, Say Nothing exercise. Maybe you will find some comic relief and inspiration and gather a bit of courage as you embark on your own personal journey.

Coming Undone

My kids seemed untethered a bit over the last few days. They pitched big, over-the-top tantrums over relatively small things. It's like they are missing the boundaries that have been set for them with all the prompting, reminding, and directing I was doing. Truthfully, I thought I would breeze through this week because I wasn't screaming and yelling and threatening. But I can see now that trying to corral my kids is just as dangerous to the relationship I have with them and their ability to develop what Vicki calls their "mental muscle." In the long run, I'm understanding that having the freedom to make their own choices—good, bad, or indifferent—will result in them being more confident, independent, and functional adults.

One Day at a Time

This is hard. And I realize I have to take it one day—heck, one situation—at a time because otherwise I just may give up. I have seen a side of my daughter that I had not seen before. Her noncompliance is usually minor, comparatively. It takes the form of noodling or minor "fits" that are easily "controlled." I do not want to control my daughter. If I can control her, so can someone else, and that's the last thing I want. Much of what she did and said this week has taken on an air of challenge, which is normally absent. It occurs to me that she doesn't trust herself to make choices because we haven't shown her that we trust her to make them. The challenge in her voice and attitude tells me that she wants to play a major role in her life and my job is to step out of the way and help her figure out how to do that.

Dishes Pile Up in the Sink

Wowie, Wow, Wow. I just came back from staring at a day's worth of dishes piled up around my daughter's placemat (she is responsible for taking her dishes to the counter and she knows it). She sat and ate dinner surrounded by old, icky food. I keep telling myself "You need this information." *Pass the duct tape!* Not quite sure how this is going to go down when hubby gets home. He will *not* like the dishes/food left out... I'm just trying to see how far she'll let it go. Wish me luck! Well, isn't this something. My daughter knew what to do with the dishes, but without all my direction, prompting, and reminding, she was paralyzed. I interpreted her paralysis and reliance on my prompting as her being uncooperative, lazy, etc. On day four she got up from the table, told me she couldn't wait for me to tell her what to do, and slowly started to clear her spot. I tried to jump in and "help," but she shooed me away—with some force, I might add—and said she would do it herself. Two hours, a cup and a half of Dawn dish soap, and one very wet and happy kid later, I understand just how dangerous assumptions are. I recognize that it doesn't really matter whether the house is messy or the kids stink or they eat crummy food and stay up too late for a few days, nothing "bad" will happen if I step back and reevaluate what's going on in the family. I know now that I can truly create a home environment that is based on mutual respect, cooperation, personal responsibility, joy, fun, connection, and love.

Love the Legos

My son has been into Legos for a while now, and got some for his birthday, so he and I were taking the time to put them together yesterday. I was really just sitting with him drinking my coffee and chatting. Every now and then I would walk away to do something, while he just plugged along building the toy and following the directions. When he got stuck on the directions the first time, I resisted my urge to tell him what to do and I just sat quietly and watched as he figured it out on his own, and so it went. It was a completely peaceful and joyful experience with him—over Legos! As I sat there watching him figure out all the little bits on his own, it occurred to me that this is a very basic example of how the Do Nothing, Say Nothing week works.

Here We Go!

We are in day four of Do Nothing, Say Nothing with two sons, ages eight and six. This week has proved very interesting so far, with immediately less stress in the house, dramatic decrease in fighting between kids, kids seem to know the basics of what needs to get done in the morning and evening routines, but they get easily sidetracked with the computer or television and then decide to "just skip it," like breakfast, homework, bathing, and cleanup. We have noticed that at bedtime there is too much television or computer and the older son is just determined to stay up as late as possible and to take over all electronic devices, and the younger son is trying to keep up (although he made his own choice to go to bed earlier last night). I am sensing that my older son is enjoying the feeling of being up later with the adults and maybe needs to have a different bedtime expectation from my younger son? We are noticing that my older son is ready for more responsibilities/ privileges than my younger son and that he needs us to recognize that.

We have definitely been impressed by our sons' abilities and also recognize areas to improve in. I feel truly empowered and supported in the way I would like to parent for probably the first time since my kids were born!

Emily Is at Choice

And finally, here is the conclusion to our story about Emily, the whiner we were introduced to in chapter 1, as told to me by her mom:

When Emily arrived at her first day of first grade, she brought out her best whiney voice—again. After all, it worked so well in kindergarten, and there was no reason to think that it wouldn't work just as well in the first grade to keep the teacher's attention focused firmly in her direction.

"Mrs. Koehler, my mom says that I should ask you..."

Before Emily could finish her sentence, Mrs. Koehler walked by her and greeted another student.

"Hello, Henry," Mrs. Koehler said, shaking his hand. "Welcome to first grade. See if you can find your name and then you can sit down and organize your desk."

Emily was confused. Why wasn't Mrs. Koehler talking to her? She tried again, only this time she whined in a more convincing tone and a louder voice.

"Mrs. Koehler. Um, well, my mom, she thinks that it would be a good idea if..."

Again, Mrs. Koehler walked by Emily and greeted another student in exactly the same way she had greeted Henry.

At this point, Emily became distressed. She counted on her whiney voice to engage the adults in her life, but it wasn't working to engage Mrs. Koehler. If she couldn't rely on her whining to get Mrs. Koehler to acknowledge her, what would she do? She watched as Mrs. Koehler greeted several other students. She stood quietly. Finally, without really thinking about what she was about to do, she looked at Mrs. Koehler and said, "Mrs. Koehler, my name is Emily and..."

Mrs. Koehler looked into Emily's eyes, smiled, stuck out her hand, and said, "Emily, it is so nice to meet you. Welcome to your new classroom."

For the first time in Emily's life, she was at choice. Emily was in a position to decide for herself whether she wanted to be a child who whined as a way to engage people, or not. Because Mrs. Koehler ignored the whining, Emily was able to choose for herself who she would be.

When mom came to Emily's first conference, she told Mrs. Koehler that she knew Emily was still whining like a baby and that they were working on this at home.

Mrs. Koehler's replied, "I am surprised to hear you say that. Not once has Emily ever spoken in a voice other than what I expect any student to use in first grade. I have noticed that when you come to get Emily, she begins to whine. However, I don't believe this is Emily's problem, I believe it is yours."

Huh? thought Emily's mother, So at home, she puts on the annoying habit, but at school she doesn't use it at all? This was the aha moment Emily's mother needed to get beyond the weed-and-water cycle. She decided to act like the teacher and pay no attention to her daughter's whining. It took all her will to zip it (duct tape came in handy) and refrain from the lecture, the commentary, the callouts. If Emily whined, she pretended she didn't hear it. Within weeks, the behavior that had run their relationship evaporated. Emily didn't need it anymore and mom wasn't expecting her to be the whiner.

It didn't happen overnight, but with new thinking and a revised strategy, Emily's mother successfully banished the weed that was causing stress and distracting her from having a healthy, happy relationship with her daughter.

Ready. Set. Go!

These are just a few of the hundreds of stories from parents who found the courage to step back, tape their mouths, and use the time to watch, learn, and access what was really going on in their families. You might be surprised to find that you can take a hands-off approach to your parenting and things will not collapse as you first suspected. This, in and of itself, will help you find the courage necessary to invest in a radically new way of parenting that has you stepping back and your kids stepping up to life.

Remember, by committing to this exercise, you'll join thousands of other parents and will have the chance to:

1. Recognize what *you* are doing to interfere with the relationship you have with your kids and how much you are impeding their ability to develop into independent, self-sufficient, cooperative, responsible, respectful, and resilient people.

2. Understand that your kids are listening to you and are willing to help out. They are paying attention to the life lessons you are trying to teach them. All they needed was a chance to show you, and staying quiet provided them the space to step up.

3. Accept that going back to this strategy again and again as your kids change and grow will provide you with facts that make it possible to maintain a hands-off approach to parenting.

4. Feel more optimistic about what's possible for you and your family, and show more faith and trust in your kids. This creates a family atmosphere of trust, encouragement, and love.

5. Begin to reclaim your own life—and everyone knows a happy mom or dad makes for a happy family. Plus, you are modeling for your kids that life isn't supposed to revolve around the kids.

6. Realize that your kids will begin to trust that they can talk to you without you going ballistic, jumping in, and trying to solve their problems for them.

The point of this week is to observe and to learn. A little craziness goes a long way in breaking through faulty assumptions and putting some perspective and balance back into our parenting. Eventually, mornings will be calmer, more fun, and more organized. Life will be easier and less stressed. You will smile more and yell less with each passing day. And you will watch in wonder as your small children slowly turn into amazingly cooperative, responsible, respectful, loving, relaxed kids.

If you are wondering about other parenting strategies you might employ, keep reading. The rest of this section offers alternatives that work in creating harmonious homes that foster independence, mutual respect, and cooperation, and that have you out the door on time most mornings without tantrums or tears.

8

Duct Tape for Your Body: Quitting Your Job as the Maid Is a Solution

> Taking care of yourself and making a positive contribution to the group in which you are a part are the biggest influences on developing healthy self-esteem.
>
> —*Vicki Hoefle*

> You can be the maid or you can be emotionally available to your children, but you can't do both.
>
> —*Vicki Hoefle*

As I discussed in chapter 3, being the maid is not an effective way for parents to promote independence, responsibility, or mutual respect in children. I pointed out some of the myths and the good intentions behind mothers and fathers who want to do it all perfectly. In this chapter, I'll talk about the many benefits to kids, to parents, and to the family when you quit your job as the maid. I will also let you know how to do it without throwing your home and your life into complete chaos. By the end of the chapter, I think you'll see why it's worth it to *stop* saving, doing for, or making life easy for your kids.

How Did I Get Here and Why Am I Wearing an Apron?

As I've mentioned, it's not uncommon for parents to wake up one day and find they are more maid, short-order cook, laundry worker, chauffeur, law enforcement officer, and referee than parent. In an attempt to keep their families moving forward, keep their homes looking tidy, and keep children out from underfoot, they fall prey to this silent enemy. Often it's a matter of parents thinking that doing for the kids is an expression of love and a parent's responsibility; sometimes it's a matter of parents wanting to be in control, needing to be needed, or thinking they will be judged by others based on their kids' appearance and actions.

No matter how a parent ends up as the maid, breaking the cycle can be tricky unless you have a clear picture of where you are going and how you are going to get there.

I'm going to guess that, over the years, you have tried systems and strategies to get your kids to help you around the house. You've tried stickers and charts and wheels that turn. You've tried bribes and praise and treats. And when those don't work for more than a day or two, you resort to nagging, reminding, yelling, and threatening. And although you can get your kids to help out once in a while, you know there has got to be a better way. I am here to tell you there is.

When my kids were little, I was determined to find or develop ideas, systems, and strategies that allowed me to solve the problem of a messy house once and for all, train the kids for their future independent lives, and enjoy them as they experienced the day to day ups and down of life.

Here is how you can quit your job as the maid without losing control of the house or your mind; it's a training system that will work with kids ranging from birth to eighteen years of age.

Duct Tape Moments

If you hear the words "good job" come out of your own mouth, pay attention and keep the roll within reach: you'll likely have to use the duct tape to plug the praise that comes dribbling out in mindless moments. There is no point in telling kids "good job" on repeat, autodial, and without any real reason other than to let the kids know you're happy with them. This habit plays into the "getting kids to" do stuff via "external motivators" cycle—just like the dangling carrots, bribes, stickers, and all that other nonsense. Once you train yourself to quit throwing "good job" their way, try replacing it with "so you did X" or "What was that like for you?" They might look at you funny but, yes, that's a good thing!

A Timeline for Training: Eighteen Years at a Glance

The Timeline for Training is a tool I have been using for more than twenty years. It is a visual representation of the time we have to train our kids, as well as a helpful reminder of the optimal times for specific types of training. With this timeline, you'll see what tasks your children can and could be doing at certain ages, when their focus shifts, and how to shift your training accordingly. You'll see that, along with tasks, we are also considering lessons that are the foundation for a satisfying and successful life. The Timeline for Training tool will show you why it's time to duct tape your hands to your side, invite the kids to help out, and watch as the magic unfolds.

When you think about it, we have eighteen years to teach our kids everything they need to know before they move out on their own. Think about your own life here. How many tasks and activities do you juggle on an average day? When we set up a system that continually invites kids to participate in their lives and the life of the family, combined with a system of training that is respectful, realistic, and reliable, our kids are far more willing to help out on a regular basis.

Here is how it works.

Here is how it works.

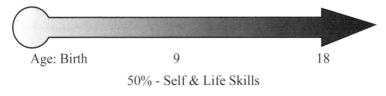

Age: Birth   9   18

50% - Self & Life Skills

FIGURE 8-1

This simple visual shows that, technically, by the time our kids are nine they have the ability to handle 50 percent of all the self and life skills they will be expected to handle in adulthood. Just for fun, if I asked you to gauge where your child is today on the graph, could he do half of everything expected of him at age eighteen? This includes everything from getting up on his own, organizing all his gear for school and sports, packing his own food, cleaning a kitchen, a bathroom, and a bedroom, handling laundry, and making meals. Mind boggling, when you think of it this way! Most parents tell me that their kids are nowhere near the 50 percent mark (even parents of five-year-olds can see clearly that they are doing too much for their kids).

When They Can Do What, and Why

One of the reasons this visual tool is so powerful is that it points out the optimal time for training. There is an ideal time to train for self, life, and social skills. If you realize this, you will see eighteen years as three smaller, clearer windows of time where learning is easier and more enjoyable for the children, as well as for mom and dad. If self-skills training is too late in the game or social training is overlooked, parents will experience stress and pushback from kids. Trust me, it is both fun and rewarding to take advantage of these ideal times and watch as your kids become more independent and happier human beings.

It's important to remember that, no matter what age your child is today or what stage of the training process you are in, it's never too late. You just might have to account for some internal and external pressures that will affect the ease of the transition!

Birth to Age Nine: Life Skills and Self Skills 101

At birth, our children are completely dependent on us for their very survival. Knowing this is not sustainable, they spend childhood learning to become independent and self-sufficient. They teach themselves how to roll over, scooch across the floor, kneel, crawl, stand up, and walk. And they do this with little or no assistance from us. As they make their way to their feet, their opportunities expand, as do their interests. Suddenly there is more to learn, and their curiosity and drive to master new challenges and tasks increase. Unfortunately, it's at this time that well-meaning parents step in, slam on the brakes, and send the message to their eager and enthusiastic kids that mom and dad will take it from here. Talk about a crash-and-burn scenario.

Children are innately interested and open to learning basic self and life skills, and if allowed and encouraged to do so, they grow into confident people who know they matter within the family and within the community. This, in turn, affects how they develop socially. By the time they are teenagers, if they've mastered basic self and life skills, they can focus on developing their social skills. Often, as parents, we can't see this progression clearly because we're too close.

It's important that parents remember kids are *interested* and *eager* to learn. Taking advantage of this eagerness and willingness to learn is our job. Letting our children practice, even if it's messy, is our responsibility. Giving them chances to fail is our gift to them.

Skills and tasks kids can learn and master between infancy and nine years of age include:

Self Skills	Life Skills	Life Lessons
• Getting up on their own	• Setting the table	• Organization
• Taking a shower or bath	• Doing laundry	• Time management
• Making breakfast	• Vacuuming	• Following through
• Organizing homework	• Learning how to cook	• Taking responsibility
• Making beds	• Unloading dishwasher	• Creating routines
• Washing hair	• Stacking wood	• Identifying personal preferences (bath or shower)
• Drying/styling hair	• Cleaning the bathroom	
• Packing backpacks	• Creating menus	
• Organizing their time	• Cleaning the kitchen	
• Brushing teeth	• Preparing lunches	
• Getting dressed	• Making grocery lists	
• Remembering sports gear	• Answering phones	
• Cleaning their room	• Making appointments	
	• Helping with bills	

Age Ten to Age Fifteen:
Plugging into the Social Circuit

When kids enter adolescence, which happens between the ages of ten and fifteen, learning how to clean their room, organize their stuff, or master the laundry aren't as important or interesting as they once were. Their focus shifts outward, toward the world, to developing and mastering social skills. This is perfectly natural because social skills are just as important in the development of our children as learning how to take care of themselves and help out around the house. Here is a short list of the social skills our tweens and young teens are learning and the life lessons that will enrich their lives and prepare them for the adult world.

Social Skills	Life Lessons
• Making friends	• Empathy
• Saying no	• Compassion
• Saying yes to an invitation	• Acceptance
• Asking someone out	• Respect
• Breaking up with someone	• Communication
• Making apologies	• Conflict resolution
• Fighting for what they believe in	• Time management
• Talking to a teacher about a grade	• Prioritizing
• Making phone calls	• Resiliency
• Making appointments	
• Listening	
• Sharing feelings	
• Accepting those who are different	
• Accepting themselves	
• Defining their identity	
• Exploring new interests	

Age Sixteen to Age Eighteen: Rebooting into Real Life

Then, suddenly, just as quickly as our children shifted their focus from family to friends, they shift their focus again and realize, "Hey, I am leaving home in two years and there is still so much I have to learn to do." Here are just a few of the things our young adult kids are interested in learning:

Life Skills	Life Lessons
• Buying a car	• Organization
• Dating	• Time management
• Getting insurance	• Follow through
• Finding a job	• Taking responsibility
• Opening a bank account	• Creating routines
• Balancing a budget	• Identifying personal preference (college or work)
• Planning a menu	• Empathy
• Cooking	• Compassion
• Choosing a college	• Acceptance
• Deciding where to live	• Respect
• Handling offers of drugs	• Communication
• Handling offers of alcohol	• Conflict resolution
• Taking positions on moral and ethical issues	• Resiliency
	• Courage

So you see, if we use the Timeline for Training to create a system that supports our children in their natural rhythm for becoming more independent and competent in the areas of self skills, life skills, and social skills, we can eliminate the fighting, the reminding, the pushback, and what some people refer to as defiance.

Imagine Your Child at Eighteen

With the Timeline for Training, we are working cooperatively with our children to empower them and to invite them
to become more independent with each day, until finally they
arrive at age eighteen ready to cross the threshold into their
lives as young adults. As parents, we can feel confident knowing we have prepared them for this journey. And our children
experience us as supportive allies who have made it possible for
them to be excited about the journey ahead.

Imagine that you invited, trained, supported, and acknowledged your children as they developed their basic self skills
and life skills for the first nine years of their lives. Imagine
how they will feel about themselves. Imagine the confidence
they will have in their own abilities. They experience themselves as responsible and capable young people who can take
care of themselves and who help out around the house every
day. They work with you, not against you. They are engaged
and harmonious, and they know they are capable of what the
real world will throw at them.

Now imagine the opposite. Imagine a child who *wasn't*
invited to participate in life as a young child, but was nagged,
reminded, lectured, and threatened into helping out or was
never allowed to do anything for himself because his mom
and dad wanted to make life easy for him or wanted things
done perfectly so they took care of everything. Imagine how
much less confident this child is as he enters his teen years.
Imagine how vulnerable he is to the influence of others and
how his lack of confidence could begin to impact his friend-
ships, grades, and willingness to try new things and explore
new areas of life. Imagine his reaction as his parents began to
demand that he pick up after himself and help out around the

house, something he hasn't done or been allowed to do until now. He begins to withdraw or becomes rebellious and questions his ability to manage his life and questions his parents' faith in him.

Clearly, if you've stopped to imagine this, you can see there is a benefit to training your child to become independent and capable, contribute to the family, and make decisions at a very young age. There is plenty of reason to back off and give happily any opportunity you can provide for your child to take the reins and steer her own life, even if she makes mistakes or sometimes fails in her attempts. Yes, she will fail, but that's how she'll learn!

You Can't Quit Overnight

Turning the reins over to your children and providing them with greater opportunities to do things on their own takes time. Training is a process. You can't just wake up one day and say, That's it, you're on your own, I'm going to eat bonbons in the kitchen. This is not at all what this method is about! This method is about a gradual, intentional shift in which you decide that your child can handle more, day by day and week by week. You know that while you're not physically there to do everything anymore, you are there to offer encouragement and help guide her if she gets stuck. You're also not there to judge, be critical, or say *I told you so* when she forgets something or screws up her schedule. This is a very emotionally active yet physically passive shift in your parenting. You keep your hands "duct taped" to your side while offering support in other ways.

To quit your job as the maid without losing your mind (and your kids at the grocery store) you must:

1. Assess the kids' skills.
2. Invite your kids to participate.
3. Train your children in skills they need to develop.

Step One: Assess the Kids' Skills and Discover What They Can Do

Take the next two to three days to assess:

- What your kids can do and will do
- What your kids can do but don't do
- What they can't do because they haven't been trained

In those two or three days you may not coax, remind, nag, bribe, threaten, plead, beg, or scream. Grab the duct tape and place it over your mouth. Not a peep from you.

You have to *watch* and document what's going on in your house, because it's the only way to get accurate information.

Is life going to be out of sorts for a few days? *Yes.* Is the house going to be a mess? *Yes.* Are your kids going to be confused? *Yes.* Will you all get over it? *Absolutely.*

Here is what I know. Parents *think* they know what their kids can and can't do. But I am here to tell you that by the end of the third day, you will have learned things about yourself and your kids that will blow your mind.

Grab a sheet of paper and make three columns.

In column one, keep track of everything the kids do on their own with no assistance from you, and I mean *no* assistance from you.

In column two, write down everything the kids can do on their own, but don't do. This might include hanging up their coats, unpacking their backpacks, making their beds, putting clothes in laundry baskets, loading the dishwasher. Again, remember this is with no prompting from you. Just watch, observe, and take notes.

In column three, write down everything the kids cannot do for themselves because they haven't been taught. This list may be fairly long, but don't get discouraged. Before long, everything from column three will end up in column one.

What Your Kids Can Do and Will Do!	What Your Kids Can Do but Don't Do!	What Your Kids Can't Do Because They Haven't Been Trained

Step Two: Invite the Kids So They Will RSVP "YES!"

This is about more than just "inviting them" to pick up their junk or learn how to empty a dishwasher. You are inviting your kids into a process that will last a lifetime.

I consider extending an invitation to a child an art form. And most of the parents I work with are in the habit of telling their kids, not inviting their kids. And kids don't like to be told what to do any more than adults do.

But here is the thing: parents are nervous about inviting their kids into this process because they expect the kids to say no. When this happens, parents feel stumped and they panic. They wonder, *Now what? I invited, they said no, now what am I supposed to do?* The easiest and best answer they have is to resort to demanding, dictating, begging, nagging, reminding, and threatening the kids to help.

Here is a disclaimer, just in case some of you are

nodding your heads, thinking, *No way is my kid ever going say yes.* I want to be totally up front with you. Don't expect the kids to jump at the first few invitations. Remember, they are used to the old dynamic and kids are naturally suspicious of all of their parents' new ploys and quick-fix strategies.

Your kids may look at you, mystified, and wonder what you are up to. *Why aren't you yelling at me? What's going on around here?* This is great, this is just where you want them. Your kids are paying attention. Allow your kids to be cautious and to test you by saying no. It isn't personal and it isn't an indication of what is possible.

I have coached thousands of parents through this process and 95 percent of the time they are successful if they allow for the time it takes and are committed to long-term change, not just to kids who will pick up their junk for a day or two.

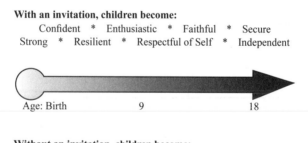

With an invitation, children become:
Confident * Enthusiastic * Faithful * Secure
Strong * Resilient * Respectful of Self * Independent

Age: Birth   9   18

Without an invitation, children become:
Uncertain * Easily Manipulated * Nervous * Rebellious

FIGURE 8-2

The Art of the Invitation

Sending out an invitation is an art form. Here is how you master it:

• **Choose the time to begin a conversation with your child with care.** Make sure you are feeling encouraged, supportive, calm, and patient. Take into account that you may have to have this conversation dozens of times, and don't expect your child to be able to digest everything you are saying all at once. Give it time. Let your child know that there are three reasons you decided to train him on how to run a home:

1. He is leaving home eventually and it is your job to ensure he doesn't have to move back home with you at twenty because he doesn't know how to manage his life.
2. It's the only way to ensure that you will not continue to nag, remind, lecture, scold, or threaten him about helping around the house.
3. If you want me to spend time reading, throwing the ball, making art projects, and building Legos with you, then I have to have some help because I can't do it all. So would you rather have me be your Mom (or Dad) or your maid?

• **Brainstorm (with your children) new skills or tasks they are ready to learn or master.** When you include your child in this brainstorming activity she feels listened to and validated and you get good information about her level of confidence and interest. It could be that you and your child generate an extensive list of ten, fifteen, or twenty skills she wants to master. And it could be that your child only comes up with one or two tasks. It doesn't matter. It's the process that matters.

• **Ask don't tell, demand, need, nag, and so on.** Ask your child which task he wants to learn or master first. He gets to decide. Asking instead of telling is what brings parents and kids closer together. If you start making demands or saying things like, "I think you need to learn this one first," you are going to get pushback from your kids and the entire process could stall out. Make sure that you follow your child's lead. Even if he chooses something simple, go with it. You are going to start with what he wants to do or what he seems excited to learn.

• **Invite, and set a new tone for your communication.** Finally, invite your child to take the lead in this process. Instead of demanding and insisting, inviting will increase a child's willingness to say "*Yes!*" Imagine what it will sound like when your kids start inviting you instead of demanding and insisting. Inviting allows children to stay in the "choice" mode, which is a powerful place for all of us to live.

Step Three: Train Your Kids and Keep the Duct Tape Handy

Training is about more than telling your kids how to do something. It is a system. A thoughtful, commonsense system for training kids to take on more responsibility in their life. Here is my Training Mantra—*Acknowledge, Build, Teach, Maintain.*

Training kids is simple if you have a plan that will support them from age two through eighteen (and beyond). As you follow your plan day in and day out, you not only establish healthy habits for the kids, you also create habits that define your family. The power of your plan is based completely on your kids, on how much they are already doing on their own and ensuring that they will keep doing things on their own.

When you have a plan that makes sense, you can track the progress your family is making and feel inspired and confident that you are parenting from a very intentional, thoughtful, and powerful place. No more guesswork.

When it comes to making a plan for your child, you'll use

your master list (from the "assess the kids' skills" step) to create a plan and implement the training. However, because no two kids will ever have the same needs, let's use an example to demonstrate how training works.

Sample: Training Lucy, Age Four

Lucy is four years old. Here is what her mother noticed after three days of observations. This is the information mom will use to create a training plan just for Lucy.

What Your Kids Can Do and Will Do!	What Your Kids Can Do but Don't Do!	What Your Kids Can't Do Because They Haven't Been Trained!
• Gets dressed on own • Makes toast	• Brushes teeth • Sets place at the table • Takes dishes to dishwasher	Self Skills: • Makes bed • Combs hair • Packs backpack • Takes bath • Gets up with alarm clock Life Skills: • Wipes table after meals • Feeds dog • Cleans kitchen sink • Helps load dishwasher

Use the Mantra, Mom and Dad

It's easy to forget that kids need a simple, consistent system to follow if they are to master all the tasks and skills required to live rich, satisfying lives. Refer to the Training Mantra as often as you need to help you stay on track.

1. Acknowledge—*not* to be confused with praise! Over the two- or three-day observation period, mom noticed that Lucy could do two things all on her own, with no support from her. She could get dressed on her own and make toast.

Mom starts the entire training process by acknowledging what Lucy can do.

Notes on acknowledgement: We are a society focused on pointing out what's wrong or still needs work. We seldom teach ourselves to focus on and acknowledge the progress and improvement our children make each and every day. Now that you know what your kids can and will do, it's important that you begin to anchor these skills by acknowledging them on a regular basis. Notice I didn't use the word *praise*? That's because praising children does not work, and there have been enough studies to suggest that praise and phrases like "good job," with a pat on the back, offer no value and only make children seek adult approval instead of recognizing their own growth.

Acknowledgement inspires kids. It sends the message to them that you see that they are actually doing quite a bit (even if they aren't yet), that you appreciate it, and that it makes a difference to you and the rest of the family. And yes, this is the biggest motivator in our kids' lives. It isn't stickers or praise or treats. For them, it's knowing that they play an important role in their family and that their family counts on them.

From now on you will begin to focus on the positive. You will move away from all the criticism and negative talk and your kids will begin to look forward to your feedback, instead of running from it. The kids will be influenced by this new language, this new appreciation you show when they do something for themselves or for the family.

To children, this "noticing the positive" feels so good inside, but it's not because you are praising them, it's because they like the way *they* feel when they help out. And they will begin to show appreciation for you and for others when someone does something for them. Hmmm. You mean, you will be living with children who have a sense of gratitude instead of entitlement? You bet! And because *they* feel good about what they are doing and about getting feedback from those most important to them, they begin to see themselves as capable and cooperative people. They like that feeling and they want more of it. It's *self-motivation*, and that is the strongest motivation there is. And before long, they begin *asking* to learn how to do more. To summarize:

- Acknowledge your children's accomplishments: *I see that you picked out your own outfit today.*
- Bring attention to their abilities: *Those tights can be tricky and you pulled them on all by yourself.*
- Ask them to talk about *how* they learned to do these things: *What did you do first? How did you know how to do that? What part was difficult? How did you solve that? What part was really simple? What would you do differently next time? What would you do again?*
- Once they master a task, there is no need to discuss it again, merely move on to the next new task.

2. Build—what can the child do but doesn't do all the time? Work on that next! In column two is the list of tasks Lucy can do, but doesn't do without reminding or nagging from mom. Mom has noticed that, among other things, Lucy can brush her own teeth and set her place at the table, but she doesn't do this on a regular basis. Brushing her teeth and setting her place haven't become habits yet. Because a child already possesses some competency with the tasks in column two, training is easier and less stressful for the child. Because success comes rather easily, the child's confidence increases and she is more willing to take on increasingly difficult tasks as you proceed.

Mom starts by inviting Lucy to talk about what mom has noticed (*I noticed that you can set your place at the table, but that you don't always do it*), and asks Lucy if she would be willing to do it every morning and evening? In fact, mom says how about they make a spot for Lucy's dishes and glasses on a low shelf in the kitchen so she doesn't have to ask for help all the time.

Remember that inviting Lucy into a conversation on a weekly or biweekly basis and asking her to decide what new skill she would like to learn is going to ensure that she feels respected, included, and in control, and she will be much more likely to be open to this new process.

3. Teach—ask, show, and let her try!

First, mom asks Lucy to show her what brushing teeth and setting her place at the table look like, so she has accurate information. This will help mom break training into small, manageable steps, so Lucy feels encouraged and can experience success. Let's say that Lucy does everything but put the cap back on the toothpaste and rinse the spit out of the sink. Mom will show her how to put the top on and how to rinse the sink.

Then, mom and Lucy agree on a time each day that Lucy will perform this task. In this instance, it will be easy because brushing happens two or three times a day and setting a place at the table might happen two times a day, but happens before another event (eating) can happen. Mom will use this as an opportunity to anchor this learning, so that Lucy begins to connect the dots. She begins to understand that taking care of herself and helping out the family happens every day and often happens during the same time of day.

To summarize:

- Allow kids time to practice and improve.
- Go slowly and be consistent.
- Focus on one or two new tasks until the kids have mastered the task.

As a parent, you will continue to step back and out of your child's life, handing the reins over in small increments. But you will be there to guide and support and offer assistance when needed. Your kids will play a more active role in their own lives, develop responsibility, and build on their success. They will gain much-needed confidence. Remember, they are getting life training that will serve them in creating a meaningful, rich, and engaged life.

Because you have a plan and your kids trust you and you are asking them to participate, the teaching and training becomes something everyone looks forward to. Soon enough, you are helping train the kids for bigger things in life. They begin to connect your help in training them with increased independence, and for this they are thankful. Instead of demanding perfection the first time, the entire family begins to realize that learning anything new takes time and support, so expectations are more realistic.

As your child masters skills, move them from column two and three to column one. Continue to acknowledge, appreciate, and celebrate progress and improvement for those column a skills.

Remember, you are going to spend time with your kids doing something. You can spend it nagging, reminding, lecturing, fighting, and bribing or doing for them. Or, you can spend it training, encouraging, supporting, and teaching your children to become contributing members of the family. You can spend it helping them develop strong self-esteem and become increasingly independent and self-confident. The choice is ours as parents.

The cycle of training repeats itself over and over again. Eventually, everything from column two is moved to column one. The only thing left to do is tackle column three. By now, you have confidence in yourself, your kids, and the plan, and suddenly the entire process is one that is enjoyable and fruitful.

4. Maintain—don't rip off the duct tape and reach back in. Give it time and keep growing! All that's left is a plan for how to maintain the system over time. As Lucy becomes more independent and takes on more responsibilities, it will be easy for mom to let up on the training. This is a common pitfall, and it happens largely because it becomes clear that Lucy is doing far more for herself and her family than her peers are and mom begins to wonder if she is expecting or perhaps demanding too much from Lucy.

I want to assure you that there is nothing more thrilling for children than to know, deep down inside, that their parents believe in them, have faith in them, and see them as capable human beings. Will there be times when Lucy's enthusiasm for taking on more responsibility wanes? Of course. In those moments, take a step back. Otherwise, keep moving forward, maintaining the system that has brought you this far.

- Be really careful that you don't slip back into your old habits. It's easy to do when you begin to notice how much your kids *can do* and how little their friends *are doing*.
- Keep expectations clear and consistent. Expect kids to forget and to give you a bit of pushback now and again.

This is part of the growth process. Remember that it isn't personal.

- Keep growing with your child. An increase in fighting among the kids usually means the kids are ready for more responsibility. And, I have to say, kids can do so much more than we parents give them credit for.
- Keep looking for "what's next" and think outside the box. Kids are interested in so many things and we tend to overlook the simplest tasks (changing a tire, creating menus, paying bills, planning vacations).
- Keep talking about how important their contributing to the house is and how much you count on them. Everyone wants to know that they are needed, important, and contributing to a successful family life.

Once you begin to train your kids, you pass the baton to them and they begin to learn how to use this system. They learn patience and the importance of practice.

Here's what the training process looked like for my oldest daughter, Hannah, and myself. I started this with Hannah when she was two. My motto is, "If they can walk, they can work." I will use helping in the kitchen as the example of the task.

At two, helping in the kitchen meant that Hannah carried her cup to the table. Four weeks later, she carried it to and from the table. Eight weeks later, she carried her cup and her plate to the table.

By the time she was four years old, Hannah could set the table for the family. It wasn't perfect, but it was by the time she was eight. By the time she was six years old, she could load and unload the dishwasher. At seven, she could and would set the table, clear the table, load the dishwasher, unload the dishwasher, and wash the dishes.

By the time Hannah was nine years old, when she chose a

task to help the family for the week and she chose "Kitchen," it meant that we could count on her to set the table, clear the table, load the dishwasher, start the dishwasher, wash the dishes, put them away, and wipe down the counters by the time we left for school.

Are my kids exceptional? Well, yes and no. They are exceptional to me, but they are like every other child on the planet in most regards. Perhaps the biggest difference between my family and other families was that we had a plan that grew with Hannah. In fact, she developed the idea that *everyone* in her family helped out each and every day, without complaint (or at least no complaining 90 percent of the time), and she discovered that cleaning the kitchen didn't really take all that long once you got the hang of it. Because everyone else was doing something to help out and people were visiting with her as she cleaned up, it didn't seem like such a big deal. I didn't have to tell her, "It's not so bad once you get started"; she figured it out all on her own.

If you are rolling your eyes at this story, let me just tell you that I have thousands of these stories from other parents who will tell you the exact same thing. It's a system. It makes sense. It's easy. It's fun. Everybody wins. And I don't know one kid who hates cleaning a kitchen more than they hate the constant fighting about helping out that goes on in the home. Quitting your job as the maid might just turn out to be the best thing you ever do for yourself, your kids, and your family.

Parents, Remember This

At the end of day, parenting is about more than just *not* feeling overwhelmed, *not* feeling overworked, and *not* feeling stressed out because you are doing too much for your kids. And it is about more than having kids who will pick up after themselves. You know that by quitting your job as the maid, by inviting your kids to participate more fully in their lives, by taking the time to train them, support them, and acknowledge all the progress and improvement they make day in and day out, you are creating the perfect environment for raising capable, cooperative, responsible, respectful, and resilient kids whose relationship with their parents is solid, trusting, and loving.

When you commit to quitting your job as the maid (and keep your mitts off your kids' business), what you are really saying to your kids is:

- I have faith in you.
- I believe in you and your abilities.
- I believe that you are ready to become more independent.
- I believe you can handle a little bit of frustration as you learn new things.
- I believe you will overcome setbacks and disappointments that you experience.
- I believe you **have what it takes** to participate in life in a deep and meaningful way.
- I believe that at your core, you want to be a contributing, cooperative member of this family and that having a parent who is lecturing and nagging and reminding you is as distasteful to you as it is to me.

Kids who have been invited to participate in life are talking with you instead of at you, or ignoring you altogether, and this is what builds the kind of relationships between parents and kids that will weather any of the storms that come with raising children in the twenty-first century. And best of all, our children become the stewards of their own learning.

As a parent, you can decide to either be the maid to your

children or you can be emotionally available to them, but you can't be both. It's time to throw down the aprons, quit your job as the maid, and make yourself emotionally available to your children, (which requires rolls of duct tape in order to break all the habits we have unconsciously created).

Why Quit Your Job As the Maid?

Here are just a few reasons to hang up your apron:

- Kids *deserve* a chance to learn how to take care of themselves.
- Everyone likes knowing she makes a positive contribution to the group she is a part of; "everyone" includes children.
- No one likes to be treated like he can't take care of himself or learn new things, especially children who are developing a sense of self-worth.
- Bored kids make trouble, busy kids do not.
- Kids are moving out and will be on their own at eighteen. It seems reasonable that we allow them ample time to practice navigating life from the earliest possible age.
- Being emotionally available to the changes, challenges, and successes of our children is the definition of parenting, not doing things for them that they could do for themselves.

9

Duct Tape for the Eyes and Ears: Ignoring the Drama and Mischief Making Is a Solution

Always make the audience suffer as much as possible.
—*Alfred Hitchcock*

Parents consistently buy tickets to attend the same bad three-act play.
—*Vicki Hoefle*

Now that we understand and can accept that we may, in fact, interfere, "do for," and interact in a variety of less-than-healthy ways with our children, we can look at this next dynamic that causes unnecessary stress and frustration and implement a simple, yet powerful solution for turning things around—or in this case—closing the curtains on the three-act play that unfolds day after day in homes across the country with mom and dad as the audience and their child in the starring role.

Free! Front-Row Tickets to the Show Starring "That" Child

Here is what this cheap drama looks like to the real world.

Have you ever been strolling through the grocery store at around 4:00 in the afternoon and witnessed a small three-year-old on the ground throwing a major temper tantrum? You watch as the tantrum escalates and the child throws herself deeper into the performance. And if you continue to watch, a scene plays out in which mom drops to one knee with a calm smile, a pleasant voice, and a reassuring hand as she enters the drama.

1. Mom is still calm, but feeling the stress rise. "Shelly, I know that grocery shopping isn't very fun, but we don't have anything for dinner, so we really need to get a few groceries. Mommy needs you to get up and be her big girl, so we can finish the shopping and go home." Nothing.

"Shelly, you have two choices. You can either stand up like a big girl and help or I will pick you up and put you in the shopping cart. Which one?" Nothing.

"Shelly, I am going to count to three and when I get to three, if you are not up off the ground and walking with me, then I am going to have to pull you up and it is probably going to hurt and then when we get home you will not have your television time." Nothing.

2. Mom is not so calm, but holding it together. Let me say here, that by now the voice, face, and attitude of the parent has changed from calm and collected to frantic and frenzied. Let's continue.

"Are you listening to me, young lady (said with clenched teeth and a plastered-on smile)? You stand up right now and stop this nonsense or you are going to time-out when we get home. Do you hear me?" Nothing.

"That's it. Get up right now!" (Mom grabs hold of the child's arm and begins to yank her up, which only increases the screeches from said child).

3. That's it! You're in trouble, or here's a bribe, kid. It's at this moment, as the child is yanked up to her feet, that the parent tries a last-ditch effort to bring the performance to a halt by using a quick-fix solution. Mom either softens her approach and says, "Listen, I know this is a drag, but we have to finish, so how about we go back to the bakery and you can get a cookie, but only this once" (the bribe), or she says, "Listen, I am going to send you to your room when we get home and if you don't want it to be worse, I suggest you knock it off right now" (the threat).

From there, this performance ends in any number of finales:

- Mom and child rush out in a frenzy.
- Mom is angry that the child ruined the outing.
- The kid is tear-stained and sniffling in the cart.

It's not fun for mom, the child, or the awkward scattering of spectators. Yet, most everyone has been here at one point or

---

Duct Tape Moment

If you feel you and your child are about to slide down the rabbit hole and into a public battle of wits, then learning this hard duct tape trick is a must: remove the negative emotion bubbling up inside of you and stick it in the car, in your purse, to the wall—anywhere but on your face and your attitude. Before the next outing, make a plan and let your child know that if he chooses to make mischief, you're "out of there" and you'll try again another day. Then, if the child does choose to test you, you can remain as cool as a cucumber as you stick that frustrated, overtired, "I'm about to lose it" negative emotion into the trunk of the minivan.

another. Still, there's a level of defeat that follows mom as she composes herself and moves along with her day.

I'll admit, never once, in all the many dramas I've witnessed, did I see it end in a satisfactory way, for either the parent or the child. Whether it's at the grocery store, on the soccer field, outside the schoolroom door, in a doctor's office, during a visit to relatives, while trying on new shoes, when putting on a heavy winter coat, while slathering on sunscreen, or any of a thousand other scenarios, the tantrum is draining for everyone involved. It's clear that parents are completely entangled in a mess, emotionally and often physically, by what I call "cheap drama."

As hosts on my favorite cooking shows like to say, let's "deconstruct this scenario" and see if we can uncover what's really going on, find a solution for this temporary upheaval, and explore some long-term strategies that might work to alleviate the problem entirely.

Behold the Three-Act Play! Next Time, Let's Skip Straight to the Intermission

Maybe you have been the unfortunate parent who feels held hostage by your child's untimely stage debut, and have found yourself knee-deep in the drama before you realized what was happening. This is tricky footing, and I often refer to this moment with a child as the "slippery slope."

Act One: Engage and Entertain—We Know Where This Is Headed

If you have been here, you know when it happens—a tantrum can come out of the blue or be prompted by a transition or a change of pace, or may happen any time your child has a different opinion than you do. One minute things seem to be moving along nicely, then suddenly you see your child's attitude and voice shift. You notice that he is getting upset, frustrated, fidgety, mouthy, demanding, disgruntled, agitated. You do your best to cut the impending drama off at the pass, but your usual list of Band-Aid strategies doesn't seem to be working, and in a split second your child is on the ground or under the chair or running away or whatever it is he does when he finally commits to the performance. And the stage is set.

Act Two: Audience Participation Makes Everything Worse

There is absolutely *no* reason to try and talk a child out of whatever he is doing (having a temper tantrum, acting shy, whining, whimpering, showing off, acting like a clown, etc.) other than to save *yourself* the embarrassment or inconvenience the child is causing you or is about to cause you. In fact, whenever parents start to step in and meddle, I ask, *Why exactly are you trying to stop a child from throwing a temper tantrum?* Tantrums don't hurt anyone. Nothing bad happens. The tantrum itself is embarrassing but, in effect, it's something that, without an audience, does not exist! So, what could be over in a matter of minutes usually ends up taking much longer (and causing far more emotional stress) once a parent decides to talk the child out of her behavior, to employ Band-Aid tactics, or to try reasoning with the child. All this attention just makes everything worse!

Test It and Find Out: Walk Away

Here is a sure-fire way to find out if your kids are performing for you or if they truly are melting down into a puddle of incomprehensible mind mush and do, in fact, require your assistance and attention.

At the next sign of a meltdown, simply walk out of the room. If the child follows you, well then, you know the performance is for you. If he yells louder so you can still hear them, it's for you. If he screams louder, then storms in to get you to react, yes, it's for you!

However, if the child continues without looking your way, then maybe he really is in distress. This would be a reasonable time to try giving a big hug and a kiss. I know the thought of taking on your lap a kid who just threw, or is in the middle of, a hissy fit puts most parents over the edge. Consider this: the child who needs to be on your lap the most is the one you least want to put there. When children throw temper tantrums, it is the best solution they have to the current problem, and remember that, up until now, it has been working to either keep you busy with them or to get them what they want. If you want your child to change, you must change your thinking, your assumptions, and your actions. So go ahead, try a hug and see what happens. Your child may relax her body, soften into your arms, and let out tears of relief.

Test It and Find Out: Who Wants Ice Cream?

The other option is to throw a mid-freak-out curveball, and declare, from left field, "I *really* need an ice cream cone. Wish I had somebody to go with me!" and see how long it takes your munchkin to dry the tears, put on the shoes, drop the clown act, and focus in. If he stops and straightens up (note: this is not a bribe, but a full 180 from where you were going), then you know it was for your engagement. Remember, emotions last only seven seconds. If you don't believe me, consider your most frustrating moment and how angry you can be and act. If, during that moment, you heard that your child was missing or your dog was hurt, would you hold onto that anger or let it go? It's the same thing here. Your child just needs something else to think about and if he's easily distracted out of the anger, it's not real.

If he doesn't respond, repeat with hugs and kisses.

Act Two takes parents from the audience and drops them center stage as they become part of the performance. Their reactions and interferences, lectures, bribes, threats, pleas, and willingness to throw in the towel and succumb to the demands of their puffy-eyed child take on more energy and intensity. They are committed to seeing the tantrum through to its end, trying desperately to stop it but with no clear direction or much confidence that they will get there. By the time it's all over, everyone feels pretty lousy and a bit foolish. And it's a sure bet that mom or dad isn't feeling a big sense of accomplishment at handling the latest performance of cheap drama any better than they did the day before.

Act Three: Bravo! An Award-Winning, Inaccurate Portrayal of Real Life

After the first and second acts, there is a third act, in which parents take over the stage, put on the mask, and participate in a healthy dose of pretending that this is how the real world will respond to their child's shenanigans.

At no time in our child's life will *anyone* other than mom and dad put up with this kind of over-the-top, drama and spend countless hours employing creative techniques to try and *talk* a child off the stage and back into real life. In fact, the real world is much more likely to keep moving, ignoring some performances and taking a detour around others.

When we engage in the cheap drama, when we act as if it's our responsibility to make things okay for the kids, we are saying to the kids, "Hey, you can expect this same indulgence from everyone else in the world, my darling," and this is just not true. No one will indulge kids in their attempts to hold people hostage by engaging in cheap drama. The truth is, anyone else witnessing a child having a temper tantrum, myself included, will merely step over them and wish them well. They won't waste a minute of their time on the dramatic tactics. Oh, sure, we wish the child wasn't so unhappy, but we all know deep down that nothing "bad" happens as a result of a melt-down, other than the parents being inconvenienced or looking like they can't control their kids.

The truth is that the job of every parent is to adequately represent to their children what they can expect from the outside world if they behave in certain ways. Offering a full-time audience is not an adequate response to nonsense, cheap drama, or other such behaviors. And again, it becomes a case where we're trying so hard to *stop* the chaos that we, in fact, set a stage for the behavior to continue! (Can you see the resemblance to watering the weed?)

Next time you're about to go there, think, WWWD? What would the world do? Hint: just keep it moving.

Close the Curtains, Already! Why Is This Show Still on the Road?

In all my years of working with families, I can say confidently that there are five primary reasons (there are others, but these come up over and over again in my work with parents) parents are still buying a front-row ticket to the performance that can only lead to disaster.

Encore presentation brought to you by the following beliefs:

1. I do not think it is okay for me to ignore my child when she is throwing a tantrum. It is unacceptable and it is rude to other people. It sends the message that it's okay for her to behave this way. *The truth is, you feel like others will think you don't know how to get control of your little hooligan!*

2. It is completely irresponsible for a parent to leave small children in a dangerous situation, and throwing themselves

on the ground can certainly be considered dangerous. In all likelihood, the child is going to hurt himself or hurt someone else. It is the responsibility of parents to get involved and help children figure out a more appropriate feeling and proper behavior. *The truth is you feel stupid because your child is flailing around on the floor looking like a fish out of water, negative feelings and emotions make you incredibly uncomfortable, and children who misbehave in public must be stopped at all costs.*

3. It's a bad idea to ignore kids when they are in the middle of a meltdown, because they don't learn to come up with other solutions to their problems. *The truth is that nobody is thinking clearly in the middle of a meltdown, and there isn't any chance that anyone will come up with any solution at all.*

4. Oh, for goodness sake, what are people going to think of me as a mother if they watch me just stand by as my child uses potty talk in public. *The truth is, you are worried that other people will judge you harshly, which is why you feel you absolutely must get involved.*

5. My child really needs help in these instances, and walking away from him would send a message to him that I don't love him. *The truth is, you don't want your child mad at you and who knows what might happen then; he might cause a bigger scene. Your attention at least gets him to quiet down.*

Break the Cycle:
Family Intermission from the Mess

It's nearly impossible to break the cycle if you haven't shifted the way you think about the cheap drama being played out by kids, so if you need to, go back and read the first part of this chapter.

Remember!

- Cheap drama isn't malicious! Kids are great actors and they have you following the script right to the final credits.
- The more you reach with the hook to pull your child off-stage, the more "the show must go on!"
- Lookers and judgers will not matter in five minutes, so don't give them the glory of you worrying about their opinions. They just don't matter. They're getting a show either way. In one show you can look a little embarrassed but unrattled, and in the other you can be just as involved as the child, earning best performance by a supporting actor.
- Once you commit to *stopping* this cycle, you're going to open up many new ways of communication. As you cut off one of your children's methods for getting your attention, they will have to find new ways to engage your interest.
- Removing any emotional attachment, visible distress, or physical response to this type of behavior allows you to stay emotionally "clean" and at the same time emotionally available to the kids and see the situation with more clarity.
- Clear your head and believe, no matter what others say, this is truly cheap drama. Once you say it out loud and adopt the thinking, it's so much easier to refrain from attending yet another bad performance.

Exercise: Get the Duct Tape, Honey, No More Drama for Me

When you're using all the energy you can muster to stay out of cheap drama, it's helpful to have a quick-reference list of what to do to keep yourself on track. Here are five solid ways to use duct tape as a conceptual tool to keep your keister out of the three-act traveling show!

1. **Ignore.** Duct tape over your ears. What? I can't hear you, and I'm not emotional about it either.
2. **Opt-out.** Stick your mom jeans to the chair and do not help, even though your child is freaking out. She will do it herself.
3. **Feet on the floor.** Tape your shoes to the floor; do not walk over there and do not get involved!
4. **Close your lids.** Tape those eyes shut. (Warning: I'm not being literal here; that would hurt and would result in serious loss of eyelashes!) That show over there is not worth viewing!
5. **Stay cool.** Tape an icepack to your neck. If you start getting heated, even without saying anything, you're involved. Stay cool, mom. Stay cool.

Beyond the Duct Tape Method supports, here are some time-tested ways to ensure you're not going to get that Oscar for best supporting actor.

- **Clever, left-field distraction.** "Oh, I forgot to tell you something. Would you look at that? Wait, wait, did you already ask me _____? Hey, I just remembered where I put the laundry detergent!" Go off topic, every time.
- **Headphones!** I used to dance around listening to music with headphones on when the kids would start their bickering. Before long I could distract them into getting their own music going and the cheap drama performance was averted.
- **Excuse yourself.** Say, "You know what, I need a moment." Go to the bathroom, or bring wine or tea or whatever you can, then sit and enjoy!

- **Stop.** Say, "Hey, I know you are in the middle of something, and I don't want you to stop, but I'm going to go kiss daddy. I'll be back in a second." Continue on to make out with husband. That will end any show, every time.
- **Stop, drop, and go out for ice cream.**

Walk over, away, upward, or underground. Simply keep moving away from the stage. If it follows you, take it outside, into the garage, and back to the porch. Eventually, your children will be annoyed and walk away!

Keep these visuals close by the next time you feel the call of the curtain rising. Use them as a reminder that you can choose not to participate. Yes, your children will get louder and try harder, but eventually, it's just not going to work for them anymore and they will gladly give up their dreams of becoming Academy Award–winning actors for a more positive connection with you.

Kids are incredibly flexible and have the ability to stop once they realize their current tactics don't work! They *only* employ cheap drama in order to:

- Solve a simple problem. They want your undivided attention and the best way they can get that attention is to play shy, throw tantrums, be confused, noodle around, or act the clown.
- Show you how much power they have in the family. After all, as soon as they begin the performance, all eyes are on them and they are in control of what happens next.
- Get back at you or hurt you for some hurt they feel you've inflicted on them. Embarrassing a parent in public with a stellar performance of "out of control kid" is a sure way to get back at a parent who has inadvertently hurt the child by believing he needs to be fixed or that he is incapable, or by treating him like a baby, or by making all his decisions for him, and so on.

• To get out of doing what everyone else in the family is doing. Maybe the child feels she can't live up to the standards the family has or she lacks the confidence to ask for help or she is tired of being criticized. Unable to articulate those strong feelings of uselessness, she resorts to cheap drama as a way to deflect attention away from her inadequacies and onto her performance.

When we start to examine the purpose of the cheap drama and allow ourselves a moment to reflect on what's happening before us instead of jumping in with both feet, which tends to make things worse, we get a clearer picture of how to be of real assistance to our kids. This insight provides parents with new options and possibilities for helping kids learn to solve problems, deal with frustrations, and find new ways of connecting with parents without the need for a meltdown performance. When parents are able to distance themselves and look at the situation with fresh eyes, they are able to see the message the child is really sending to them.

Duct Tape Diaries: Real Parents Walking Out of the Theater

Here are some true tales from parents who checked out of the audience and left the theater before the three-act performance got underway.

Ignoring

It took me a few weeks to muster up the courage to step over my child as he was in the throes of a temper tantrum, but it was just a few days before the tantrums started to go away. A year later I have a four-year-old who wouldn't think about even attempting a temper tantrum, and when he does, the only thing it tells me is that he is completely overwhelmed, frustrated, or exhausted and just doesn't have the resources to deal with the situation. At that moment my empathy and understanding kicks in and when it does, I am able to kneel down, look into my child's eyes, and say in a calm, thoughtful, and loving voice, "I get it. We are done for now. Let's go home." I use these temper tantrums now as beacons that inform me how my child is doing rather than looking at the behavior as needing to be "fixed." Do I still get the hairy eyeball when it happens? Sure. But I don't care because the look on my son's face removes every other face in the room.

Cover the Lids (Look Away)

Recently, my kids, six and three years old, started fighting with each other at lunchtime. They continue to pick on each other and pick at each other's food. It is inevitable that one starts to fall apart or retaliate by really ramping up and becoming mean. I used to engage by buying into this picking and talking to them about being nice to each other. When that did not help, I would threaten with a loss of privileges. When this did not help, I would try to separate them and have one eat at the counter and one eat at the table; this would make the yelling louder, as they would scream at each other across the room. I would eventually lose it and start to lecture, yell, and dramatically toss their food in the garbage and banish them to their rooms until further notice. This really meant I sent them away until I calmed down and started to feel guilty for my reaction.

A few days ago, when all was calm and before we had lunch, we all talked about what was happening at lunchtime and we worked out an agreement on how to handle this. After I proposed several ridiculous solutions, they decided that if they started to fight at mealtime I will move them to opposite ends of the table. If the fighting continues, the meal is over for them. We all shook hands and congratulated ourselves on a good agreement.

The next day the fighting began again at lunch. Without a word I moved the kids to opposite ends of the table. The fighting continued so I picked up their plates and gently tossed their sandwiches in the trash. My six-year-old daughter, shrieking, threw a bunch of bananas on the floor and then ran into the living room and pulled all the cushions off the sofa and was screaming at the top of her lungs.

I went about my business and straightened up the kitchen and invited both my children to join me for some cookie making in the kitchen. I was quiet and did not say a word. The screaming from my daughter eventually stopped and she quietly came in and asked if she could put the next ingredient into the bowl. Of course I said yes, and we spent the next thirty minutes mixing, baking, and eating cookies.

I am happy to report that for the past week, we had pleasant meals with no fighting at the table. The interesting part (well, maybe it's obvious) is that the fighting overall has diminished. I am getting practice at ignoring the fighting, following through on agreements, and moving on to the next event. No lecturing, no yelling, no sending them away, no emotional drain, and no attention to the fighting or, in Vicki's words, cheap drama. I feel like in the real world, people would either get up and move themselves out of the room if two people were fighting or they would ignore it and go about their business, and that is what we are trying to create.

Opt Out

I have a daughter who uses her "shy" act to get me to engage with her and it drives me mad. I've tried everything. We've talked about shyness ad nauseam. And nothing I say makes any difference or impacts my daughter's ability to overcome her "shyness." I finally decided that if I didn't want to cripple her for life I was going to have to do anything I could to eliminate the cheap drama and commit to not falling prey to her antics. We were at a carnival one day and someone gave her a wand with ribbons on it. She didn't even make eye contact with the man, let alone say thank you, which got me going. As the man walked away she looked up at me and said, "Mama, I want the sword with the diamond in it. Will you go ask the man to trade?" I paused for a moment and collected my thoughts. She continued, "I'm too shy, Mama. You do it for me, okay?"

This scenario plays out in our daily lives over and over again and it never ends with any resolution or with either of us feeling connected, encouraged, and more confident about what we will do next time. If I wanted to break the cycle, I was going to have to do it now. I said in my most loving, empathetic, and firm voice, "No, I will not go over and ask the nice man to trade the wand for the sword, but you can walk over and ask him yourself." The shock on her face was evident. I had never said anything like that to her. After the shock wore off, she hit the floor in a crumpled-up ball, put her hands over her head, and began to wail. You can imagine what everybody watching us was saying. "Why don't you just go get her the sword? What's the big deal?" "Just do it this once. It's not like this is going to happen again anytime soon."

I know everyone was trying to help but this was exactly what I feared. People looking at me and thinking I was an unfit mother or an unsympathetic mother or, even worse, a completely disconnected, mean mother.

I was so tempted to step in and try to talk to her, to make her stop wailing, to just give in and go ask the man if we could trade the wand for the sword, but I knew how it would end once I entered the drama. She continued and repeated over and over again, "I'm too shy. I can't do it. I'm shy." I remember Vicki telling me that there would be a moment when I could decide what message I wanted to send my child. I could either hold her in a state of faith and believe that she could do it, or look at her as a cripple who needed my help. Those were powerful words for me. I stooped down and I whispered in my daughter's ear, "If you want the sword you will have to go and ask the man for it, and if you decide not to, that's fine, but I'm not doing it for you. The choice is yours."

I stood up. I had no idea what was going to happen, but my heart was racing. To my surprise, my child stopped whimpering. She looked up at me and we locked eyes and I remember thinking, She's going to choose the shy act again, but instead she stood up slowly, grabbed my hand, looked at me and said, "Not today, Mama, maybe next time." I realized at that moment that staying out of the cheap drama, that recognizing I was making things worse each time I saved her or tried to talk her out of her shyness or put her in a position where she would have to be assertive, I was only making things worse. When I offered her the choice and I communicated to her that I had faith in her, she suddenly started to experience herself differently.

Vicki called me about six weeks later to ask how things were going. I told her honestly that we were making progress. I also told her that it would probably be years before this child truly experienced how courageous she could be after all my years of meddling, but that I was completely committed to helping her on her journey. This one little strategy has completely shifted our lives. Without it I would have distanced myself from this child. I would have started to judge her shyness as a ploy to keep me engaged. I wouldn't have taken any responsibility for my part in the drama. Was it hard at the beginning? Yes. Was it worth it? Absolutely.

Stay Cool

My child plays the helpless card. "Mama, Mama, can you help me with my shoes. Mama, can you help me put the toothpaste on the toothbrush. Mama, I can't do this by myself, will you help me. Mama, this is too hard for me, I need you to come help me. Mama, I forgot what to do, can you come show me again?" This went on day in and day out.

When Vicki first suggested that this was cheap drama and that I was being duped by a smart kid playing helpless, I had a hard time believing her. His helplessness seemed so real to me. Can you imagine a mother actually walking away from a child who's asking for assistance? But as Vicki began to play out the scenario, I recognized that I had indeed been hoodwinked by my clever little thespian. My child knew exactly how to get me engaged with him. She suggested this one strategy that changed everything in our lives. The next time Josh asked me to help him, instead of beginning our usual game of hide-and-seek around the helplessness, I walked over to him, made eye contact, and said "Show me what you can do first."

The look on his face was priceless. He had no idea where this storyline was going to take us. I had never said anything like this before, and Josh was completely caught off guard. I said it again, "Josh, show me what you can do and then I will show you what to do next." And at that moment I saw the light flicker behind his eyes. He was tentative, to be sure. This was uncharted territory for both of us. All of our connections and most of our interactions during the day were over his being helpless. He had no idea where this might lead and I recognized that in the moment. This realization helped me stay calm and centered—a far cry from my craziness that usually followed his tenth, "Can you help me, Mama."

Believe it or not, the task he was working on was putting his jacket on and zipping it up. The funny part was, he didn't even have the jacket on but he was already anticipating his inability to zip the zipper. I realized then that in many instances he just assumes that he can't do something. So I walked him through it. I said, "Can you pick the jacket up?" He looked at me and said with indignation in his voice, "Of course I can pick the jacket up." A smile escaped both of our lips. I said, "Can you put your arms in the sleeves?" He said, "Of course I can put my arms in the sleeves, Mama." This continued until we got to the zipper. By that time he was ready to try it by himself. I didn't even ask, "Can you get the right side of the zipper into the left side?" He sat down and said, "Before you tell me how to do it, Mama, let me try." My heart melted. I realized that all this time what he'd really been saying is, Can you show me how to do the next step? But we'd gotten ourselves in this cheap soap opera of *I can't do anything without you, Mama.*

It's been three years now and the difference between the little boy he was back then and the young school-age child he is now is the difference between night and day. I know other parents were watching me with wonder and with judgment as I started to change my response to Josh's requests for help. His helpless act had defined our entire relationship. Unraveling that and reestablishing a relationship that was built on his being capable and competent didn't happen overnight. It was a long haul. But, as Vicki likes to remind us, *What else have you got to do that is more important than helping your kids experience themselves as strong, capable, resourceful, and resilient human beings? Unless, of course, you like paying top dollar for a show you've seen a hundred times and decided after the first showing that you didn't care for. In which case, buy another ticket and have at it.*

A Final Checklist: Cancel the Show Forever

Kids are trying to tell us something with their behavior. Instead of watching the show or jumping onstage with your kids, get the duct tape, stay out of the performance, and consider other influences that can be addressed in other ways:

- It could be that the time of day you're trying to accomplish a particular task is the worst possible time for your kids, and a little rescheduling will solve the problem entirely.
- It could be that your kids need to be spending time with you in other more positive ways. Remember that if they don't get a solid connection with you, they will take any connection.
- It could be that they don't yet have the mental muscle to deal with frustration, disappointment, waiting, rejection, unfairness, and boredom. This will take time. In fact, it will take many years of practice. Consider yourself your child's personal trainer in the development of resiliency, flexibility, and adaptability.
- It could be that their outbursts are clues and signposts to a deeper problem. Maybe the relationship needs a bit of repair, or maybe more training is required; consider that possibility, instead of looking at the outburst as a behavior that needs to be "fixed."

Once you commit to closing the curtain, you're going to discover that the drama subsides and you can see from a new perspective, one without a microphone, spotlight, and stage. Take the time to take notes, and recognize when you have consciously decided to remain disengaged. Give the method time and stick with it, because things will get better! All you have to do is keep that duct tape handy!

10

Prepare for Departure: Launch with Enthusiasm

To reach a port we must sail, sometimes with the wind and sometimes against it. But we must not drift or lie at anchor.

—*Oliver Wendell Holmes*

The real success of parenting comes from knowing that our children will throw open the doors at eighteen and walk into their lives with confidence and enthusiasm.

—*Vicki Hoefle*

I believe that it is our responsibility as parents to ensure that our children throw open the doors at age eighteen, pause, turn, take one last look at us, and, with a smile on their face and excitement in their eyes, cross over the threshold and step into adulthood with confidence and enthusiasm. If this is to happen, it is essential that parents shift their view of parenting from a hands-on, quick-fix, micromanaging, damage-control approach to a hands-off, intentional, proactive relationship-focused approach.

Eighteen years isn't a lot of time when you consider *all* the things our kids will be required to do when they leave our homes (see chapter 8). Doesn't it seem reasonable that we take advantage of every opportunity, every learning situation, and every experience possible to invite our children into their own lives and give them time to practice navigating the ups and downs life provides each of us on a regular basis?

Imagine the confidence, excitement, and enthusiasm your children would experience if they were given the chance to "practice" navigating the ins and outs of everyday life with your guidance and support.

Imagine how *you* will feel, knowing that you prepared your children for the most *important* part of their lives—life beyond your threshold. Holding on to children as if they are ours—pretending that they will be with us forever—is indulgent on our part and is a disservice to our children. It is not about pushing them toward adulthood, rather it's about showing them how to get there confidently.

What Are Parenting Roadmaps?

Parenting Roadmaps offer a powerful, easy-to-use tool for tracking where your family is today, where you would like it to be in a week, a month, or a year, and how to use the strategies introduced in earlier chapters to reach your goal. Roadmaps are used to create family mission statements that help instill values in children and help them develop healthy habits that will last a lifetime. They are used to assist children in identifying changes they would like to make in their own lives in the areas of academics, athletics, social life, and community, and to prepare them for life beyond our thresholds.

Roadmaps take those monumental changes we want to make in ourselves and in our families and break them down into manageable, measurable, realistic bits, so they can be more easily applied within the family dynamic, ensuring an enjoyable journey and a successful outcome for everyone.

Roadmaps help parents realize they have time to readjust

Duct Tape Moment

Take your roll of tape and stick your family's roadmap where you can see it and study it. If you are working toward a short-term goal (ie, getting out the door in the morning) and you notice you're nagging about who left the bikes in the back-yard, it's time to put a piece of tape over your mouth. If you are working on a long-term goal (ie, raising independent global kids), cover your mouth when you get into a tizzy over your child's refusal to play in the T-ball squirt league. If it's not moving you toward your goal, cover your mouth! Other-wise, you'll be engaged in power struggles and discord in five directions.

the dynamics, which releases the pressure to "fix" kids right away. They help nurture and support steady growth that happens over time. Roadmaps enable parents to shift their focus onto the child's future and away from the mismatched clothes, lost mittens, messy rooms, meltdowns, stubbornness, and pushback we see in day to day parenting.

There are four types of roadmaps that can be introduced into your family today to bring about lasting, sustainable change. You'll find that even when you've trained yourself to take a more hand-off approach to parenting (your duct tape helped with that), sometimes a visual reminder—an indicator or guide to let you know if you're working in the right direction—comes in handy.

The Four Parenting Roadmaps:

- Personal Parenting Roadmap: Who do *I* (the parent) want to be and how will I get there?
- Family Roadmap: What do I want for my family?

- Short-Term Roadmap: How do we develop useful skills and helpful habits?
- Kids' Roadmap: Who do I (the child) want to be and how will I get there?

We're In: Now, How Do We Create a Roadmap?

To create a Roadmap, we'll use the information and thinking we've gathered from the previous chapters and create a framework that will guide us on the journey with our children. We will map out with a marker and paper all sorts of key factors to:

- Identify core values that can be used to develop a mission statement that supports, guides, and empowers the entire family and teaches children how to live into those values, even when it's tempting to squash them. *We are a family who believes in mutual respect and we show this to each other when we:*
  - *Listen when someone is talking.*
  - *Consider each other's point of view.*
  - *Find solutions that consider everyone's needs.*
  - *Make agreements and follow through.*

- Identify where you are today as a parent. *I am a parent who is frequently frustrated with my children for not helping out and as a result I find myself nagging, reminding, directing, and giving in.*

- Identify where you would like to be in a week, a month, or a year. *I want to be a more encouraging, patient, and confident parent who has a more hands-off approach to parenting with a focus on developing a strong relationship with my child and allowing her to become an independent person.*

- Identify where your children are today, no matter how old they are. *My child has difficulty in the morning managing his time and the tasks necessary to get out of the house on time. He uses temper tantrums to engage me in power struggles.*

- Identify where you would like to see your child in a week, a month, or a year. *My child is able to manage his morning with little or no help from me and has the confidence to take on new challenges with enthusiasm and a sense of curiosity.*

- Navigate the distance between where you, your child, and your family are today and where you want to be in a week, six weeks, six months, or six years.

- Set reasonable expectations so you and your kids can experience more success by making incremental changes and leveraging that success to try new things, develop new traits, conquer challenges, and work together more cooperatively and with more fun.

- Celebrate the daily progress and improvement the family experiences instead of waiting for the perfect result. *Yesterday we were ten minutes behind schedule. Today we were on time and prepared.*

- Teach your children how to set goals, identify priorities, create healthy habits, and monitor progress.

The best part is, the Roadmap is a tool you can use from the time your kids are two until they leave home at eighteen. Here is an example for you.

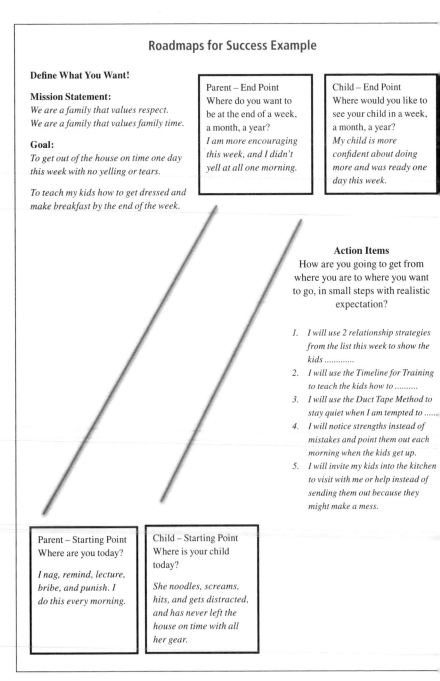

Roadmaps for Success Example

Define What You Want!

Mission Statement:
We are a family that values respect.
We are a family that values family time.

Goal:
To get out of the house on time one day
this week with no yelling or tears.

To teach my kids how to get dressed and
make breakfast by the end of the week.

Parent – End Point
Where do you want to
be at the end of a week,
a month, a year?
I am more encouraging
this week, and I didn't
yell at all one morning.

Child – End Point
Where would you like to
see your child in a week,
a month, a year?
My child is more
confident about doing
more and was ready one
day this week.

Action Items
How are you going to get from
where you are to where you want
to go, in small steps with realistic
expectation?

1. *I will use 2 relationship strategies*
   from the list this week to show the
   kids ....
2. *I will use the Timeline for Training*
   to teach the kids how to ....
3. *I will use the Duct Tape Method to*
   stay quiet when I am tempted to ......
4. *I will notice strengths instead of*
   mistakes and point them out each
   morning when the kids get up.
5. *I will invite my kids into the kitchen*
   to visit with me or help instead of
   sending them out because they
   might make a mess.

Parent – Starting Point
Where are you today?

I nag, remind, lecture,
bribe, and punish. I
do this every morning.

Child – Starting Point
Where is your child
today?

She noodles, screams,
hits, and gets distracted,
and has never left the
house on time with all
her gear.

FIGURE 10-1

Creating a Personal Parenting Roadmap

I admit it. I have dictator tendencies. And I could imagine myself as a dictating mother, which was an image I found distasteful. I knew that proclaiming "I will *not* be a dictator when I become a mother," would have been as useless as saying I will *never* have a cup of coffee again! What I needed was to decide for myself *who* I wanted to be (if not a dictator) and how I would become that person. It occurred to me that in other areas of our lives, when we want to make a change, we set goals and measure our progress, and this was the beginning of my idea to use a Roadmap to plot my course.

I started by asking myself one big, beefy question: What do I want my kids to say about me when they are twenty-five?

Imagine this scenario: Your twenty-five-year-old son comes home for dinner and brings his best friend. Maybe the friend is his college roommate, a coworker, a love interest, or a spouse. This person turns to your son and says, "In one word, describe what your mom was like when you were growing up." There is a pause. What do you want your child to say about you? Do you want him to say, "That's easy. My mom was a dictator through and through. There was no doubt that she made the rules and made sure everyone lived by them." And there you would sit, knowing that what your son said was the truth. You were the dictator. And if you could do it again differently, you would.

If you could choose a word right now—a word or phrase you want your child to use to describe you as a parent—what would that word be? For me, it was "radical faith." I wanted my kids to look at the friend and say, "My mom had radical faith. She had faith in herself, faith in her kids, and faith in the world. She demonstrated that faith each and every day."

And that's when I realized that unless I had a roadmap that would help me become a mother of radical faith, in all likelihood I would default to a mother who dictated. The choice was mine.

Here is how it works. Draw your map and then fill in the boxes.

1. Use one word to describe the parent you are today. *Dictator*
2. How do you do that word? *I boss, direct, remind, nag, threaten, and lecture.*
3. What words would you like your kids to use when they describe you to their friends? What is the final destination on this map? *My mother had radical faith.*
4. What must I do, each and every day, regardless of the circumstances, to demonstrate to my children that I am a mother of radical faith?
   - *I will use the Timeline for Training to help my children become independent, self-reliant people who are able to manage their lives and know without a doubt how much trust and faith I have in their abilities.*
   - *I will use duct tape as needed to manage my dictating ways and take a more hands-off approach to parenting, sending the message to my kids that I believe they have what it takes to overcome frustrations, work things out with siblings, and find solutions to their problems.*
   - *I will focus my attention on using relationship strategies to support my child's growth and confidence in her own abilities and to solidify our relationship.*

I knew what I had to do and now I had a way of creating an action plan for myself, a way of holding myself accountable, a way of tracking my progress and improvement, and a way to celebrate when I took two steps closer to my goal of being a mother who showed radical faith in her children. Was it easy? What do you think? But I had nothing else to do in my life that was more important than this, so it was easy to make the decision to do the work. I just needed a Roadmap to help me take the next baby step in my journey.

This was my long-term Roadmap. Once I had the big picture clearly in my mind, I broke it down into weekly mini-roadmaps that helped me execute my plan. This kept me moving steadily forward, and with each success I harnessed my enthusiasm and confidence and applied it to the next week. Did I slip up? You bet, but it didn't take me long to regroup and get back on track. You will read later in this book how my decision to become a mother of radical faith affected each of my children.

We are responsible for how our children describe us when they are twenty-five. And they will choose a word that best captures the attitude, the words, and the behavior their parents demonstrated most consistently. We don't have the luxury of turning into stellar parents two weeks before our eighteen-year-old leaves home and expect that all of the other lousy parenting traits will be wiped away. Our children will remember the daily interactions and the daily atmosphere and this will be what solidifies their image of us.

Kristin's Aha Moment

Here is a note I received from a parent who was initially very resistant to the idea of creating a roadmap, until she actually made one.

"I'll admit I didn't really get why creating a Roadmap was so important. It wasn't until I found myself doing exactly what I swore I would never do that I realized just saying 'I absolutely refuse to be the control freak' or 'I don't want my kids describing me the way I describe my mom,' is not enough to bring about change. In the beginning, I hadn't decided who I wanted to be and even if I had, I had no idea how to behave in a way that supported who I wanted to be. I had been trained to be a control freak. It's what I knew. It's how I defined myself. It's what I resorted to when I didn't know what else to do.

So, after the twenty-third do-over, I decided to create my

first Roadmap. It changed my life and the lives of my kids in ways I can't even begin to explain. I use Roadmaps for everything now. It's such an easy tool to use once you get the hang of it. I know it might be awkward at first, but believe me when I say that if every parent was taught how to use this tool, life with kids would be the amazing journey it's supposed to be and not the one we so often dread."

Creating a Family Roadmap

You create a Family Roadmap in much the same way you create your personal one. My husband and I each wrote down our top three values and began a conversation about each of these values and how they might impact our children and our family. We decided together to choose "mutual respect" as a place to start.

We made a list of all the ways that we would demonstrate that value each and every day. Because the kids were young, we chose three areas from the list to focus on. Any more than that and it could have seemed an insurmountable task to them. We wrote out a Family Mission Statement and posted it in plain view as a way to inspire us and influence our parenting decisions:

"We are a family that values mutual respect and we demonstrate this value by:

- Speaking with respect to each other.
- Showing respect for each other's opinions, preferences, likes, and dislikes.
- Including everyone in the decision-making process."

As we began to speak more respectfully to each other and developed this as the norm in our family, we added another area to work on. As the kids got older we included more ways to demonstrate our mutual respect for each other. Do you know what you get when you create a Roadmap and a Mission Statement that are based on showing every member of the family respect? You get a respectful home with respectful people who embody what mutual respect is. It's no mystery that people commented on how much respect we showed each other. We worked on it.

Sample Family Mission Statements

Here are a few examples from other families who used the Roadmap to create Mission Statements to guide their families.

Mission Statement Number One:
This Family Values Family Time

Mom and dad were both distracted with life. When they were with the kids they were distant, annoyed, frustrated, and felt disconnected from them. They wanted to change the family dynamic, but nothing they tried worked for more than a day or two. We sat down together and they created a Mission Statement and a Family Roadmap to help them make the changes that would reconnect the family and create an atmosphere of love and appreciation:

"We are a family that values family time and we demonstrate this by:

- Spending two hours each week participating in an activity we all enjoy.
- Taking fifteen minutes each day with each child to share our day and make a connection.
- Eating breakfast together three times a week."

This was a great place to start, but this couple didn't know how to actually implement these action items. We had to drill down so they could make this a reality in a family that didn't think they had any extra time to spare. Here is how they did it.

- What will it take for you to carve out two hours every week to invest in family time?
  - Mom and dad quit their jobs as the family maids and used the Timeline for Training to train the kids and redistribute the chores so they would all have more time for each other. They kept their expectations realistic, gave the kids ample time to practice, and acknowledged the progress and improvement the kids were making.
  - Mom and dad invited the children into the process of choosing the time together and what activities they would enjoy. They decided to try new things that none of them had done before, and this brought the family closer together.

- What will it take to carve out fifteen minutes each day to connect with the kids?
  - Identify times of the day that the parents allowed themselves to get distracted, and instead use this time to intentionally connect with the kids. Both parents identified three or four times a day when they could indeed spend time with the kids, and within days they were looking forward to the fifteen-minute connections.
  - Focus more on connecting with the kids and less on trying to entertain them. With this new focus, the couple realized the possibilities for *how* to connect were unlimited.

- ○ Ask the children if they would like to be taught how to use the sewing machine, the food processor, or the table saw (at appropriate ages, of course).
- ○ Stay focused on the connection and *not* on trying to teach one more little lesson when you are together.

- • What will it take to eat breakfast together three times a week?
  - ○ Use the Timeline for Training to make sure the kids feel confident and competent in the kitchen.
  - ○ Use the Duct Tape Method as needed to stay quiet and allow the pancakes to burn, the blender to overflow, and the dishes to wait until after dinner.
  - ○ Focus on relationship strategies, in particular acknowledging strengths, during the family's time in the kitchen to avoid falling back into useless Band-Aid tactics.

Joanie shared the following story with me when we met for coffee six months after her family created their Roadmap.

Eating breakfast together three times a week proved challenging for a few weeks, but it wasn't long before we began to treasure these morning meals, and now they have become a kind of family tradition. There is laughter, people are relaxed, and the kids take turns surprising us with new recipes. It's amazing. Something so simple has the power to so significantly change a family.

Mission Statement Number Two: This Family Values Trust

Mom is bossy because she is afraid of what will happen if she isn't in charge. The message she is sending to her kids is that she doesn't trust them, and at the same time she doesn't have much trust in herself when it comes to her parenting decisions. What she wants most in the world is for her kids to trust themselves, and she'd like to develop a bit of faith in herself in the process.

"We are a family that values trust and we demonstrate this value by:

- Allowing our children to make decisions for themselves that are safe and respectful.
- Saying yes before we say no.
- Proving to ourselves and others that we can be trusted by talking with each other respectfully."

Again, I worked with mom and dad to develop these action items further.

- What will it take for you to allow your kids to make decisions for themselves that are safe and respectful?
  - Use the Timeline for Training to evaluate what the kids can do that we haven't been letting them do and start acknowledging what they can do to help them gain confidence.
  - Use the Duct Tape Method to stay quiet as they develop more confidence in their abilities and to show we have faith in them and trust them and that it's okay if they make mistakes while they are learning.
  - Focus our attention on the relationship with the kids instead of using underhanded strategies to boss them around.

- What will it take to say yes more than you say no?
  - Try it and gather information that could be helpful in reframing what the kids are really capable of doing without direction from us.
  - Say yes one more time each day.

- What will it take for us to speak respectfully to each other?
  - ○ We will apply the duct tape until we can learn to hold our tongues, think about what we really want to say, and then say it in an open, honest, and respectful way.
  - ○ Speak to our kids as if we are speaking to trusted and respected friends.

Karen shared her story with a group of parents I was working with who were skeptical about the power this simple tool had at transforming the family dynamic:

Even this was too open ended for us. Vicki worked with us to create a very specific seven-day Roadmap with actionable items for us to do during the morning, afternoon, and evening. At first, we thought that this would be a completely overwhelming and burdensome process, and instead we found that as we wrote down how and what we would do, we were inspired and invigorated and we could feel the passion for our parenting return. This turned out to be the most powerful tool in completely transforming our family. Friends and family commented over and over again that they didn't recognize us. It was some powerful stuff.

Short-Term Roadmaps

Short-Term Roadmaps are useful when trying to navigate a busy life, meet your daily obligations, and raise your kids in a loving, nurturing, organized home. Here are just three examples of how families incorporated Short-Term Roadmaps into family life.

Short-Term Goal Number One: Nag Less This Week

Sandy brought the kids together for a conversation: "Here is what the morning routine looks like today. I am yelling and nagging you kids. And you seem to stall out and get distracted. At the end of the week, how would we like the morning to be? Let's make one change, do something different this week, and see what happens."

The kids agreed.

Sandy got out the Roadmap and they worked on it together.

- Mom: I will stay quiet at least two mornings this week and allow my kids a chance to step up and take ownership of the morning.
- Kids: I will take responsibility for making my lunch and getting my stuff together and if I choose to play Legos instead, then I won't be mad at Mom because it wasn't her fault that I didn't have my stuff.

Sandy added more to her Roadmap because she wanted more than to just get out of the house in the morning. She wanted her kids to feel confident and more engaged in life and she knew she would have to keep working throughout the day to ensure she got the kind of change in her family that she was looking for.

On her Roadmap she added things for her to do:

- Continue to train the kids in one new task each week.
- Keep the duct tape handy and when I am tempted to nag, remind, and yell, use it to stay quiet and give the kids a chance to figure out a solution that will work for them.
- Allow the kids to make mistakes without criticizing or correcting them.

- Find a time to connect with each child for just a few minutes that sends the message that I love them and care about them.
- Keep my focus on the relationship with my kids, not on my to-do list.
- Inform the teacher that I am raising thinking kids and thinking kids are messy and make mistakes. Ask her to support my efforts and not save the kids when they forget something for school.

Sandy took the time to write down all of these action items and each night she reviewed how she did:

I had to remind myself over and over again that if I didn't have a plan for how I was going to prepare my kids for life on their own then they would never be ready. The first few weeks were hard and I was tempted to throw the whole thing away until one of my kids, out of the blue, announced at breakfast that she was so pleased about how things were going and that she was so lucky because she knew how to do things that her friends did not.

I was hooked. We use the Roadmap for just about everything now. The kids are part of the process and, as a result, they take more ownership of their lives and they let me know when they are ready to take on more. Because I am changing my behavior, they are willing to take more responsibility for theirs.

Short-Term Goal Number Two: Get Out of the House on Time

Susan and Paul are both dictators. Both of their children are disorganized and easily distracted, or so it seems to them. They cannot for the life of them get out of the house in the morning on time with any regularity and without someone being upset.

Their long-term goal is to have calm, pleasant, and connected mornings with children who are organized and able to manage on their own so they can all leave the house on time, smiling. Their short-term goal is to leave the house calm, pleasant, and connected once this week.

Does a Family Roadmap often feed into a Short-Term Roadmap? You bet. That's the beauty of it. The Roadmap is a multilayered approach.

The goal was for the family to leave the house one day that week feeling calm, pleasant, and connected. Here is the action plan:

- Monday morning: Ask the kids to show us what they can do on their own and take notes.
- Monday evening: Use relationship strategies to focus on the boys' strengths and to make a connection with them. Use the Duct Tape Method to manage our mouths and invite the kids to come into the kitchen to visit with us or help with dinner prep if they are interested.
- Tuesday morning: Show the kids how to take over two self skills (information gathered from the Timeline for Training exercise) and then give them a chance to practice for the rest of the week.
- Tuesday evening: Notice what has been going well and acknowledge the boys for their focus and hard work.
- Wednesday: Keep going. Make connections. Notice and acknowledge improvement. Use duct tape to stay quiet and keep from interfering.

Susan and Paul created a Roadmap for the week and used different-colored sticky notes to remind them of what they were going to do each day. As they finished an "action item" they crossed it off, feeling a sense of pride and purpose in their commitment to their kids.

On Sunday evening, the family gathered together and mom and dad acknowledged all the progress they made over the course of the week. They asked the boys if they noticed anything different about the week and both boys announced, "You aren't bossing us around as much and we like that." Mom and dad shared what they noticed about the boys and how much they were doing for themselves. At the end of the conversation, they merely asked the boys if they wanted to try these changes for another week. The boys were completely on board. Mom and dad took out a sheet of paper and they wrote down what they would do differently the following week. The boys were quick to ask their parents to continue to be quiet and maybe even stay out of the kitchen, so they wouldn't be so worried about making a mistake. They agreed, and again mom and dad returned to their room to create a very specific Roadmap for the week that would help guide their parenting decisions and keep them moving toward their long-range goals.

This couple took the time to evaluate the week, build on what was working, and tweak the parts where they had gotten tripped up. They wrote a new Roadmap for the week that built on what they started the week before.

Here is what they shared with me:

Yes, I know this isn't a "sexy" way to parent. It isn't instinctual and natural and spontaneous. However, it is a framework to build structure where freedom can flourish. Structure without freedom is jail for the kids, freedom without structure is hell for the parents. The Roadmap creates balance that can be maintained for years. I'll take this over what we had any day.

Short-Term Goal Number Three:
Let the Child Get Ready by Herself

Jennifer acknowledged that, in an attempt to get out of the door on time each day, she was crippling her children's desire and ability to take on more responsibility. As a result, they had begun to fight more and her kids seemed more distracted and discouraged with each day. She wanted a way out of this dynamic and she was willing to do whatever it took to change course. Here's where they started and where they ended up.

Child's starting point: "Can't" get out the door on time.

Parent's starting point: Jennifer nagged, reminded, helped, bribed, threatened, counted, then picked child up and moved her to the car.

Child's final destination in seven days: The child was able to get herself ready and be on time once in that week.

Parent's final destination: She used her Mission Statement to help stay respectful, used the Timeline for Training to set realistic expectations, and took every opportunity to notice and acknowledge progress and improvement.

Result: They reached their goal. In Jennifer's words:

I wrote down all of the things that would help me succeed and then each time I did them, I ran into the bedroom and put it on the Roadmap. I loved the feeling of anchoring it at the moment. It seemed to motivate me to do it again, to be creative with another relationship strategy or find another way to duct tape myself out of a situation. I started looking for ways to invite my kids to help me out, or just visit with me while I was peeling carrots. Before I knew it, my kids were asking to help. It wasn't long before I was happy, smiling, more relaxed, and looking forward to running into my room to make a quick note. I kept thinking to myself, every day that I waste is a day closer to my kids failing when they leave home at eighteen. It was a huge motivator for me. I stopped focusing on changing the kids and realized that I was the power behind all the changes in the house. I love that.

Be Patient and Realistic

With Short-Term Roadmaps, it's important to create realistic expectations. Part of the reason families get caught in the cul-de-sac syndrome is because of unrealistic expectations. For instance: "I will give up *all* my nagging and my child will never noodle again and we will accomplish this in less than thirty days." We all know that isn't going to happen. When we slow down, when we create an intentional Roadmap with clear and reasonable expectations, our chances of success are multiplied exponentially. Slow, steady progress is what creates lasting, sustainable change.

A realistic expectation sounds like this: "I will cut the nagging by 20 percent and I will do this during the morning routine. My child will have learned how to take care of two things I am currently doing for him because I took the time to train him and we will only be late for school three days instead of five."

A Roadmap can also help parents answer questions like:

- Why isn't this situation any better than it was a week ago?
- What is it that is tripping us up?
- What do I have to change or consider if I want a different outcome?
- What am I doing or not doing that is contributing to a negative outcome in this situation?

Helping Kids Create Roadmaps

We worked with Roadmaps so often that our kids finally decided they wanted their own. We thought it was a brilliant idea and encouraged them to go for it.

When our kids were in the seventh, eighth, ninth, and eleventh grades, they decided to create one Personal Roadmap that would track four areas of their lives during each quarter of the school year:

- Academics
- Athletics
- Social life
- Community service

I want to mention here that the Roadmap is not a to-do list. To-do lists are static. Roadmaps are dynamic. They point the way and they make it possible to arrive at your desired destination in the time you planned, with a sense of accomplishment and joy. They also allow kids to make adjustments as needed, something a mom or dad with a to-do list might be reluctant to do. So use your duct tape to keep your mitts off your kids' Roadmaps.

Example: My Daughter's First Roadmap

My youngest daughter, Kiera, agreed to let me share the first Roadmap she made for herself:

- I want to raise my grade from a C to a B+ in math, which will bring my GPA up to a 3.8. I will do that by:
  - Finding a tutor
  - Having my brother check my work
  - Talking to the teacher if I am confused after class

- I want to get ten more minutes of playing time during each soccer game. I will do that by:
  - Running sprints, because I am slow
  - Dribbling the ball thirty minutes a night in the yard
  - Asking the coach what I have to work on and then getting to work on it

- I want to practice eating with other people at school and not just the friends I've had since preschool. I will do this by:
  - Finding a group of kids who look nice and asking them if I can join them
  - Asking someone from one of my classes if they want to eat with me at lunch

- I want to find a new volunteer project that works with the elderly. I will do this by:
  - Calling Project Independence and finding out what the requirements are for volunteering
  - Calling the hospital and seeing if they have volunteer positions to work with the elderly who are recovering from surgery
  - Talking to my neighbor and asking if I can help her with household chores or outside pickup

My daughter reached her goals. By writing them out, creating actionable items, monitoring her progress without pressure from her parents, and talking with her siblings when she hit roadblocks to her success, she was able to tap into her creative nature, develop the discipline to accomplish tough things, and cultivate the "can do" attitude she still embodies today.

It wasn't uncommon for my husband and me to hear one of the kids saying that she realized that playing on the varsity squad wasn't as important as she thought it would be and that she was happier with more playing time on the JV squad. Or that she met someone at school she really liked and that never would have happened if she hadn't written it down on the Roadmap.

At the end of each quarter, the kids would bring down their Roadmaps, we would have a family celebration, and they would share their experiences. My husband and I quickly realized that it made no difference to us whether a grade improved or whether they actually accomplished any of their goals. The real growth we saw was in their ability to access, to discern, to predict, to prioritize, to recognize, and to make adjustments in their lives. They were becoming thoughtful, reflective, curious, industrious, and resilient people, and that is what we wanted for our kids.

Today, all of the kids are out of the house and either in college or working. They live 3,500 miles from home, and part of what makes their lives work so well is their ability to return to the Roadmap and identify their goals for the coming year and know what it will take to meet those goals.

Because the Roadmap is personal and self-directed, kids are willing to do the work it takes to reach their goals, they are able to set realistic expectations, they know how to set up the necessary resources they might need in order to meet their Roadmap goals, and they know what trips them up (I didn't know what tripped me up until I was well into my thirties).

Example: A Father Helps His Fourth-Grade Daughter Set a Roadmap

With younger children, it's easier to focus on one area at a time. Here is an example where a parent helps his young child create an Academic Roadmap.

Father: Is there an area in your school life you would like to see some improvement in?

Daughter: I would say I am a C student in spelling, so maybe I could improve in this area..

Father: Where would you like to be at the end of the marking period?

Daughter: I would like to be a B student.

Father: What will it take for you to get there? What will you have to do each day to accomplish that goal?

Daughter: I would have to study thirty minutes every night.

Father: And when would you like to study?

Daughter: After dinner, because my tummy is full.

Father: And how will you remember to study after dinner when your tummy is full?

Daughter: Oh, I don't know, maybe you could remind me.

Father: No, I will not remind you, because then we will end up fighting against each other, not working together. How can you remember?

Daughter: Can we put some music on and that will remind me it's time?

Father: Yes. We can try that for a week and see how it goes.

This conversation continued until dad asked enough questions to help his daughter create a simple Roadmap for herself. She wrote down everything she would do to accomplish her goal and hung the Roadmap in her room.

Dad reported in several months later:

The first few weeks were awful. I was so tempted to jump back in and take control of her homework. I realized only after we overcame that hurdle that she was testing me to see if I would really let her take ownership of her Roadmap. Once I had convinced her I wouldn't use it against her as a way to manipulate her into doing her homework, she took complete ownership of the goal and used the Roadmap masterfully. It proved to me, once again, that my kids do care about their grades, as well as the relationships they have with their parents and siblings, and about helping out around the house, but when I butt in, when I try and take over, it pushes them out of the way and they retreat. I know now that if they retreat, it's because I am being overbearing again. This is a great reminder for me to stay in the backseat.

Example: A Kid's Bucket List Roadmap

The Bucket List Roadmap became our favorite. Here is one story (we have dozens of these, and the kids still use the Bucket List Roadmap to plot their next adventure).

Our son Colin created a Bucket List for himself shortly after his return from Chile during his junior year of high school. He knew he wanted to return to Chile, and we encouraged him to follow his heart and his dream. However, as his parents, we needed to feel confident that he had a thoughtful plan and could show us he was ready for the adventure. I want to add that he already had the financial responsibility taken care of. All of the kids were working from the time they were fourteen years old, and he knew that securing a second job might be required if he planned to travel for a year.

Colin's Bucket List read something like this:

- Start the year abroad by becoming TEFL (Teaching English as a Foreign Language) certified so that I can find employment and make money while I am abroad.
- Spend three months on an organic farm where I can practice the language, live with a family in country, work for my room and board, and become familiar with the culture, the country, and my surroundings.
- Spend three months traveling from Patagonia to northern Chile by bus.

- Secure a job in a beach resort using the skills I picked up on the farm and learn to surf.
- Spend three months in the Andes teaching English and skiing, and using my carpentry skills to make additional income.
- Make connections with people who can further my education and interest in living abroad.

Colin achieved almost everything on this list and more. He was in Chile during the recent earthquake and helped out in the hardest-hit villages. He did indeed learn to surf, he taught English and skiing, and he traveled extensively. The only reason he returned to the States is because of a knee injury. Within weeks of his return and post-surgery, he had another Roadmap underway.

Roadmaps Are Not To-Do Lists, They Are Live-It Lists

Roadmaps are more than to-do lists. They are tools, available to anyone who is looking to create an intentional life filled with meaning, fulfillment, and joy.

Are Roadmaps difficult? No, but they can be challenging as you learn to create and use them. I ask all the parents I work with, "Is creating a Parenting Roadmap any more difficult than the dictating, controlling, micromanaging, and punishing you are currently doing, or more difficult than living with kids who whine, fight, noodle, blame, and mess around all the time?" Of course not.

We are at choice. We can put our time and energy into anything we want. We can create the lives we want or we can allow circumstances to determine the quality of our lives.

It is also worth remembering that we are asking our children to try new things every day and, personally, I think it helps every parent become more empathetic and understanding if they themselves are engaged in learning new things, being challenged to think differently and to act in new ways.

If we remember that our job is to prepare our children to leave our home ready to face the challenges of life beyond our threshold and with the ability to navigate an ever-changing landscape with confidence and enthusiasm, then using a tool to help us track our journey is a logical, rewarding approach.

Why Make a Roadmap for Your Family?

The truth is that one day your freckle-faced, wide-eyed, toddling cherub will leave your home and enter the real world. The other truth is that she may or may not be ready for life beyond your threshold, or to meet the challenges life throws her way, or to take care of her needs, or set goals, or create a satisfying and fulfilling life for herself. She may or may not know how to recover from a setback or failure or come up with plan B or C or even D when life throws her a curveball. It is your job to make sure that she is ready to leave home at eighteen with the skills to walk into her life with confidence and enthusiasm.

This path to living a confident life, to knowing who we are and what we want, with the necessary skills to create and navigate our life, takes more than hard work. It takes a plan, a Roadmap; otherwise, we may just find ourselves feeling stuck, lost, and helpless.

11

Duct Tape Works: Stories from Real Kids of Duct Tape Parents

When parents commit to using their mental duct tape to break a micromanaging style of parenting for a more hands-off, relationship-focused approach, children gain the opportunity to discover that mistakes are a part of life and that they have what it takes to recover from them. They learn how to handle frustration, disappointment, rejection, and embarrassment without overreacting, blaming, melting down, or acting out.

These kids don't look to mom and dad for every answer, but look to their own inner compass for guidance before asking for assistance. They also discover what they like (turkey sandwiches, not PB&J; showers, not baths; dresses, not shorts) because their parents have trusted them with decision making (even the decisions with consequences, like not getting up to the alarm, not washing their laundry, or forgetting their lunch), and they learn to trust themselves.

Parents who trust kids to fail and rebound raise thinking, engaged, independent, cooperative, responsible, resilient, problem-solving children who have the ability to navigate the world around them with ease and wonder. These kids are willing to take risks, try new things, apologize, make amends, and participate fully in the human experience. They care about the relationships they have with family members and are willing to do what is necessary to keep these relationships healthy.

It's not easy adopting a hands-off approach to parenting with a focus on relationship-building efforts, but it's worth it. Here are real stories from real families that will inspire you to step back, allow your kids to step in, and appreciate the growth your children can achieve. They will enlighten and show you what is possible.

She Knew, I Listened—Let's Get Rid of the Diaper

Not long ago our eighteen-month-old started to react badly to having her diaper changed. Typically, I would get frustrated and muscle through it, and we'd both end the experience feeling badly. This time, I *see and hear* my little one protesting as I'm about to put on her new diaper. I stop and ask, "Okay, what?" I pick her up, put her down. She goes right into the bathroom and points to the potty. I stick her on the potty and guess what? She pees. Go figure! After we finish up in the bathroom, we put on her new diaper, both happy as clams. That experience was too cool.

A hands-off approach to parenting requires that I rethink my assumptions, that I look at my child and see the world from her perspective, and it is then that I see all the possibilities. I don't need a "strategy," I just need to tap into what is right before my eyes.

He's My Little Problem Solver

This morning my three-and-a half-year-old son was pouring milk into his glass on the dishwasher door (shout out to my mother-in-law, who gave me that tip; if the drink/cereal/ whatever spills, who cares, you just close it up!). The milk came out fast and filled his glass to the very tippy top. He set the carton down, put his hands on his skinny hips, and said to himself, "Now, how do we solve this problem?" I am thrilled that this little guy already sees himself as a problem solver, both responsible for the problem and capable of solving it.

Thank you for helping us lead this child to a place where he is taking ownership of himself and his actions at such a young age.

Train Them and Trust Them

My daughter is five now and has type 1 diabetes. Before Duct Tape Parenting, I was up in the middle of the night, checking her blood sugar to make sure it was stable. The control I needed to feel over her diabetes sometimes leaked out into the rest of her life and I didn't like that. Truth is, I don't like *me* when I parent in this controlling way. I wanted my daughter to be confident and independent, not shy, insecure, and dependent on me. She absolutely must be confident if she is to manage her diabetes and get the most out of her life.

I had to change the way I parented her and take a more hands-off approach so that she could grow and develop confidence in herself. Here is the latest story in her young life: at Open Gym she was much more creative and adventurous than she has ever been, putting together little routines and showing confidence in her ability and willingness to do them in front of others. I saw a confidence that wasn't there before. Coincidence? I don't think so.

Contributions Aren't So Bad

My kids have been enjoying their contributions so much this week. Currently, my six-year-old is experimenting with vacuum cord management, which involves jump roping. My eight-year-old, while washing dishes tonight, said, "I feel like the dishes are my children and I am giving them a soapy bath." It is so fun to see them contributing and having fun!

Clean Slate

I love how my nine-year-old has taken up the training for his little brother. He is so encouraging, empathetic, and patient. It is an absolute joy. They do a few tasks together this way, allowing for extra time for the two-and-a-half-year-old to practice.

Everyone Enjoys a More Hands-Off Approach to Parenting

This morning I overheard C and E chatting in the kitchen:

C: Why doesn't mom ever get mad at us?

E: Because she's doing the parenting class and she's supposed to ignore your bad behavior and only notice your good behavior.

This program makes sense to kids. They just get it. They don't always like it, but they totally understand it.

I still get mad, of course, but nowhere near as often as I used to. And when I do get mad, I'm much more grown-up about it now. No more flying off the handle at my kids' expense. So, compared to what they see out in the world, I'm a virtual Gandhi.

It's the Little Things

It's the little things that stand out: My six-year-old saying she always wanted to know how to make oatmeal, and now she can. My four-year-old saying it was the luckiest day in his life when we took a hammer and hung some pictures.

From Slouch to Swagger

When we started to implement a more hands-off approach to parenting in our family, we told our youngest that we had not done our job in letting him learn how to take care of himself, and that we got in the way of him developing some life skills. We told him about Vicki and her wisdom. The plan was going to be that we would let him take over the morning tasks. The first days we would spend seeing what he could do. His reaction was classic—his shoulders slumped, his eyes rolled, and a power sulk was brewing. We reminded him to let us know what tasks he needed help with. Washing grapes was his request.

The next morning, he was slouching around, packing a lunch, making breakfast, and sighing dramatically. At one point he said, "I liked it better when you were my servants." Bingo! Clearly we were not only enabling him, but disabling him. Yikes.

Then, the next day, he was snapping around with some swagger and even washed the grapes himself. The older kids, who were quite independent and competent, were feeling him getting a little more skilled very quickly and were shocked to see him packed, fed, teeth brushed, and backpack on ten minutes before the bus was due. He was all puffed up. Within several months, he was making egg sandwiches on his own, getting the pan from high up on the shelf, timing the English muffin, and flipping the egg to perfection.

The best news was how this new independence translated to the rest of his life. Some of his attention-seeking behaviors and whining stopped. He was feeling so capable and connected that he started initiating other areas where he could take charge.

This information is life-changing for everyone.

It's Not Our Routine, but Their Routine

Although the transition to them doing things for themselves was initially difficult, our kids now understand that they are doing things most kids their age don't know how to do. Even though they might not want to do their "responsibilities" at times, they like the freedom and power that comes from initiating jobs on their own, taking pride in them, and reaping the rewards they've earned.

They understand the control they have over their own lives and have the ability to make decisions for themselves that might involve mistakes. Also, they see all the other kids running to mom or dad, day by day, minute by minute, and they like the idea that they don't need to do that. Their confidence has grown in leaps due to these things.

Honestly, my husband and I marvel at them. It took a while for mistakes to happen, kids forgot lunch, backpacks, snow pants, but after a time, they established their own routines, and now mornings are some of the most peaceful, organized, and enjoyable times in our day. It's not our routine but their routine, and they have it down to a science.

Kudos from the Teacher

Today I got a call from my child's teacher and she said, "I know what you guys do at home and the independence that you foster there shows up here in the classroom. The things you guys have your kids do in the morning, like making their own lunch, gives them such self-confidence. I'm not sure what you see at home, but it's so strong here. I can clearly see the connection between the independence you give them and the confidence here at school."

Midwinter Car Accident—She Figured It Out
(In Flip-Flops, No Less!)

When my daughter was sixteen years old, she purchased her own car, paid for her insurance, scheduled her own tuneups, and changed her tires when required. She was a responsible young adult and a cautious driver.

I got a call on a Wednesday afternoon in the dead of winter from her, telling me she had been in an accident. She was panicked and scared.

"Mom! Mom! I've been in an accident!"

"Hannah, are you okay? Are you okay? Are you hurt?"

"No. No, I'm not hurt, Mom. I'm okay. But Mom, I don't know what to do."

Of course she did. We talked about what to do in case she was ever in an accident, but she wasn't thinking. She was scared and she wanted me to make it better. And I was tempted. I was tempted.

"Hannah. I am going to hang up now. You are okay. Now you have to think. You have to figure out what to do. Call me when you figure out what the first step is."

"MOOOMMMM!"

I hung up the phone. And I paced and I prayed and I knew that she would be fine. I waited.

The phone rang.

"Mom. It's Hannah." Calmer now.

"Yes."

"I have to call Triple AAA. I have to tell them that I was in an accident and I have to tell them where I am."

"Yes."

"I found the card with the number on it, but I am not sure where I am."

"Call me after you call them."

"Mooomm."

I hung up the phone. I had more confidence now and I knew she did too. I had to believe in her if she was going to believe in herself.

"Mom. Mom, I called them. I figured out where I was. I called them. They are coming. I have to wait sixty minutes, but I can do that. I have a heater in the car and I have a blanket in the trunk and I have water and I'm fine, Mom. I have flip-flops on but I'm fine. Really."

"Will you call me when they get there?"

"Yes, Mom. Yes."

"I love you, Hannah!"

"I love you, Mom. Thank you."

Later, when I was telling a friend about the incident, she looked at me with shock and probably a bit of disgust.

"How could you *not* go and help her?"

"Because," I said, "the next time I might be in Kansas and she will be in Vermont and then I won't have the luxury of hopping in my car and driving to her rescue. Now, at sixteen, she knows she can rescue herself. That counts for something."

Bear Hugs at Seventeen

Last night my husband invited our seventeen-year-old son and his best friend to join him at his weekly basketball game for the over-forty group. My son was happy to oblige.

They had a great time together, testosterone surging, a bit of bumping, trash talking each other, and the sweat flying. The time came for my son to take his friend home but some of the guys decided to play one last game. My husband waved good-bye to our son, so as not to embarrass him, and turned back to the over-forty guys waiting for him. Here is where it gets good: over walks our strapping seventeen-year-old son, who grabs his dad, gives him a bear hug and a kiss on the cheek, and says "Love ya, Dad, thanks for the invite. See you at home," and walks off into the sunset.

As my husband reports it, there was dead silence from the group. And then it came, the looks and comments from other fathers who wished that their sons would have not only the confidence but the genuine love and respect for their dads to be able to walk over and openly demonstrate that love.

How lucky am I? How lucky is the world?

I'm Cool with It If You Are

My daughter is four with blond hair down past her shoulders. Evidently, it was becoming a problem.

"Mom, I would like to get my hair cut short."

"You would? Are you sure?"

"Yes. Short like my brother's."

"Okay, I'll make an appointment."

During the haircut appointment, the stylist kept checking with me after trimming a quarter of an inch. I would direct her focus back to the child in the chair, who kept saying, "Nope, shorter."

Finally her hair was close to her head and over her ears and her grin was from ear to ear.

The next day one of her friends comes over to play and takes one look and exclaims, "Your hair looks dumb." She says, "No, it does not." The friend says, "Well, it looks stupid, then." She replies, "No, no it doesn't, it is just what I wanted."

I do not worry, even a little, that this child will be influenced by anyone. She knows who she is, what she wants, and she is confident in her decisions. What more could a mother hope for?

Seven-Year-Old Sensibility

If you had told me that my seven-year-old daughter had the courage and self-confidence to glide with grace through this sticky situation, I wouldn't have believed you. Then I saw it with my own eyes.

"Mom, why would someone not like me?"

"What do you mean?"

"Well, Emma is having a party and invited every girl (all seven) in the class, but did not invite me. When I asked her about it, she told me she was not allowed to invite me, because her parents don't like me."

"Really?!"

"But it is okay, Mom. I am still going to be her friend, because she is a good person. I was just curious what I could have done that would make her parents not like me."

The next day.

"Mom, Emma and I decided we are going to have a special lunch at school to celebrate her birthday, so I am going to give her this necklace that I made and we are going to have sandwiches together in the classroom."

When I grow up, I want to be just like my daughter.

Resilience for the Real World

A year earlier and this exchange would have been quite different. Today however, this child of mine has the kind of resilient nature that most adults long for.

"Mom, when do you think Sascha will call? I am all ready to go to the park and she said we would be leaving around 9:00. It's almost 9:00."

"I don't know, do you want to give her a call and check in?"

"No, she said she would call me, I can wait. I am just so excited to be going."

About twenty minutes later, as Janae is looking out the window, she says, "Oh, I guess I am not going with Sascha, she just drove by with her mom."

Janae buried her head in the couch for a few minutes and let out a few whimpers. I went over and sat next to her and put my arm around her back. She snuggled in and after a few minutes, she looked up at me and said, "That just does not make sense. If plans changed, it would be much better to call someone and tell them, rather than just leave them wondering."

I agreed and told her I was going to make some muffins and invited her to help. She looked at me, smiled, and said, "Yes."

This is what I call resiliency.

Honesty and Honoring Agreements

My son is my hero.

"Hey mom, Here's my driver's permit."

"Why? What's up?"

"Well, last night at Gerry's house, I had a beer."

"Okay, thank you for honoring our agreement that if you used poor judgment or broke the law, you would lose your Learner's Permit for ninety days and thank you for being honest with me. When you get home from school, I would like to sit down and talk more about your decision to have a beer with Gerry."

"Okay, Mom, I love you."

"I love you, too."

Mittens: Problem Solving Leads to Very Successful Plan B

You just don't know what's possible until you step back and watch as the magic unfolds

"Mom, can you come bring me my mittens? I forgot them at home."

"No, sorry. I can't today."

"Whaatttt?? But if I don't have mittens, I can't go out for recess."

"I know. But I trust you will be able to figure this out."

"But Moooooooom. Please."

"I love you, bye."

Later that day, "Mom, mom, mom, guess what?!"

"What?!"

"I solved the problem. I figured it out. I borrowed a mitten from Nate, and then I used Jim's hat on my other hand and the teacher said that was fine and I got to play outside."

Every time I am tempted to "save" any one of my kids, I remember the look on my son's face in that moment and tell myself, "If you jump in now and save him, you will take away the opportunity for him to experience a success and own it."

Appreciation for Teen Empathy

Every time I am feeling a bit stressed or anxious, my fourteen-year-old daughter takes me by the shoulders and looks me square in the eyes and asks, "What is going on inside of your body right now, other than pure joy and happiness? And what can I do to help you?" And then she proceeds to give me a big kiss and hug. That's it, exactly what I needed.

Jaw Dropping Conversation on Capability

I overheard this conversation and couldn't help but think how lucky I am, how lucky we are, to have found this hands-off approach to parenting. Here is my five-year-old daughter chatting with a friend of hers:

"Do you want a drink of water?"

"Yes."

"The glasses are over there."

"I can't get a glass by myself."

"Yes, yes, you can."

"No, we can't. Won't you get in trouble?"

"No, my mom teaches us how to take care of ourselves, so when we are older and move out, we will know how to live on our own."

Silence.

"Hmmmm, my mom has no idea what I can do."

"Oh, I would tell her."

"I will."

She Can Manage Both Time and Money, So Purple Hair It Is

To be honest, three years ago my daughter never would have had the courage to ask about purple streaks. Today, we enjoy the kind of relationship most mothers dream of having with their brassy, independent, and stubborn daughters.

"Mom, can I get purple streaks in my hair?"

"Sure, do you have enough money?"

"How much will it cost?"

"I don't know."

"Mom, I called the hair place and it will be about $50."

"Okay, do you have enough money?"

"I will in three weeks."

"Okay, do you want to make an appointment?"

"Yes, when can you bring me?"

We pick a date and she makes the appointment.

It Makes Sense to Her, After All It Is Her Hair

My daughters, ages five and eight, are in the bathroom for a long time, quiet. This should have been enough of a clue that something was happening.

"Mom, look what I did to sissy's hair!"

I turn around to see the long, curly, blonde locks removed, and left in their place is scraggly blonde hair, short and in places very close to the scalp.

"Wow!" Bordering on a big scream.

Thankful for the gentle reminder from my husband, "It's just hair, it will grow back."

"Yes, Mom, don't be mad. I asked big sissy to do it. Everyone keeps talking about my hair. I am sick of them talking about my hair. Now, they won't talk about it anymore."

Big smile from *ear to ear*—and, by the way, she is now seven years old and just deciding to grow her hair long again.

Is That You, Roxy?

My husband and I wake up to the rustling sounds of wrappers and drawers. I roll over to hear husband yell, "Roxy, get out of the trash can!" and instead hear our eight-year-old answer "It's just me, I'm making my lunch!" Husband rolls over. "Holy cow, he's on top of his game." We are back to bed until 7:45 A.M.

Teamwork

I hear, "Shoot! I forgot to do my laundry. Would you run the dryer for me if I fall asleep before it's done?" Five minutes, later, he's got a full load in his arms, taking it downstairs, getting it going. I'm thinking, *It didn't even occur to him to blame me for the fact he doesn't have any clean clothes!* Nice. And, of course I'll swap the load for him. GO teamwork.

My Son Doesn't Have a Bedtime and I'm Cool with That

Why doesn't my son have a bedtime? Because he wakes me up every morning shouting, "Bye, Mom," on his way out the door.

Off he goes with his backpack, boots, jacket, and everything he needs, his homework and all. I never would have guessed he could do all of that by the time he was ten years old. And so, with his morning routine in check, I say, go ahead, make your own decisions about bedtime, as long as I don't have to get you up out of bed.

Where Did I Put That Duct Tape?

Upon suggesting that my son clear the counter before spraying it with cleaner, he said, "Sheesh, I wish you weren't in here and you'd let me just do it how I want." All right, then. I exit stage left.

Turn Autopilot to Off Mode

I was so used to pouring drinks and managing snacks that I didn't realize how many times my kids came to me for something as simple as a cup or plate. Once I realized I was autopiloting, I moved all the dishes down low and put the plastic containers, cups, and snacks within reach. Now when they come home from school, I just say, "Hi," and they say, "Hi," as they walk in the door and head merrily on their own way to pour cereal, milk, snacks, and so forth. It's just so much easier.

Holding Small Tasks in High Regard

One day my daughter had a fellow kindergartener over. The little girl kept saying she was hungry. I looked around and noticed that my three kids had poured cereal and nobody noticed she hadn't. So I said, "Hey, go ahead and pour yourself some cereal! Which kind would you like?" She said, "I don't know how," and I froze, thinking, *Wow*. I said in my most encouraging voice, "Just go for it. Tip the box and pour out the cereal." She said, "What if I spill?" I said, "Look around. Nobody will care."

She proceeded to pour her cereal and literally squealed with delight. I couldn't help but appreciate all the times I'd let my kids do something as simple as pour cereal, even if it made a mess. I wondered how far on her roadmap this little girl was and saw how, even at six years old, she got caught in a lapse of confidence and I could visibly see her discouragement and apprehension, over cereal! This made me commit to holding the small tasks in high regard.

Traditions

To get us back on track with family meetings for 2012, I purchased a new notebook and H decorated it. Already we're off to a good start. We have our meeting diligently each week and she is the scribe. After she listed our appreciations the first time, she looked up at me and said, "We should keep doing these things, since we know the other person likes it."

Family Rules

During a winter carnival weekend at the high school, both the sixteen- and the fourteen-year-old chose (on their own, with no force from their parents) to opt out of the events of the carnival and spend the weekend with family members who were visiting from out of town.

Family Meeting Teaches the Value of Money

Practicing family meetings from the time my kids were five and three years old meant that each week they received an allowance to learn how to spend, save, and give away. They both knew that when they were fourteen years old and could work outside the home, they would stop receiving allowance.

Two weeks before his fourteenth birthday, the oldest was out filling out applications and looking for employment. He is happy to report that, while many of his friends think they should get a day off from school on their birthdays, his fourteenth birthday was his first day of work.

Now the youngest child is fourteen and finally found employment that she can balance with her full sports schedule. She quickly discovered that the occasional babysitting job is not supporting her budget for clothing, activities with friends, and saving for a car.

Ten-Year-Old Knows Her Limits

After a weekend of family and friends visiting, late-night bedtimes, and loads of outdoor winter activities, my ten-year-old daughter crashes into bed on Sunday night and asks if she can go in late to school the next day. I trust her and say, "Yes."

The next morning she is up at 9:20 A.M., still a bit groggy, but explains over cereal that she had math first thing and she is all caught up, but she really has to be there by 10:00 A.M., because there is a reading group and play practice that she just can't miss.

Moments later she says to me, "Mom, thanks so much for trusting me and letting me sleep in this morning."

Making Milkshakes with a Seven-Year-Old

I knew we had made progress when I could listen without getting defensive and my daughter had no hesitation in saying what she thought.

Daughter: Do we need ice?

Mom: I'm going to put ice in it.

Slluuuurrrrrrrp.

Daughter: I don't think it needed ice, but Mom, it's good that you put ice in it this time, now you know for the future, that you don't need to put ice in the milkshake.

12

Duct Tape Is Good for the Family: A Family That Works Together, Sticks Together

Taking a more hands off approach to parenting, focusing on relationship strategies, and using duct tape when our resolve weakens has profound ripple effects throughout the entire family. Once parents accept ownership of the part they play in every interaction they have with their child and commit to change, an amazing thing happens as if by magic (but we know now, it's by design).

It's not uncommon for families to undergo a metamorphosis that they might not realize they were even capable of! This chapter highlights the big picture positive effects the family experiences, including:

- Less fighting
- Long-term healthy relationships
- Peaceful conflict resolution
- Harmonious exchanges
- Organized space
- Shared responsibility
- High-functioning dynamics
- Emotionally healthy family members

Remember, change happens over time, and with your new understanding and a commitment to a more hands-off approach to parenting, you will experience firsthand the powerful change that's possible. Not every family will look the same in their results, but every family can experience improvements in areas where they currently struggle. Enjoy the following stories of trust, discovery, and new thinking.

Keeping My Mouth Shut Opened My Mind

The five days of Do Nothing, Say Nothing were a challenge for me, but it forced me to be more creative in my interactions with my daughter. I liked it! There were a lot of times when my mouth would open and I just didn't have a darn thing to say that wasn't interfering, so I closed it. And then I was forced to think about what else I could do, and whether I needed to do anything. I began to realize that many times, I really don't need to do anything. I *wanted* to butt in, to micromanage, to give a lecture, but I realized that that is very different from needing to do something, and so I learned to keep my mouth closed and my brain on and to think, not react.

During those five days of silence, I realized that I was parenting in survival mode, parenting in a way that was convenient for me, and not taking the time to create an intentional parenting plan that would support my kids. I understand now how important it is to implement new, relationship-focused strategies into my parenting plan. They will support my daughter and help her gain more control over her own life.

This Year? A Cooperation-Filled Camping Trip

We had a huge improvement in the preparation and cleanup for a camping trip, compared with the way we handled the trip last year. Last year, the eight-year-old ran off, feeling free to play as we worked like ants to pack and unpack. Even the one-

and-a-half-year-old lugged his own sleeping bag, pillow, and so on. We were so angry last year. This year, the nine-year-old was asked to come back to us after doing a task and ask, "What else can I help with?" until we, the team, were done. He resisted a little, but was met not only with a happy family, but a big independent bike ride across the campground when we were just about ready to check out. Debriefing at home included noting that we all were done faster, it wasn't an angry time, and as he practices, he will better be able to see what needs to be done, to know what comes next, and he won't have to ask. Again, as we slowed down our tasks to find things he was capable of doing, he would also look at his tasks and seek something his little brother was capable of doing, too. It was awesome.

Seeing the other families we camped with let their kids just sit there and do nothing, and then yell at them for whining and complaining, was a magnifying mirror on what we had done so many times ourselves. We have come so far. We're all making strides and are so thankful for your support, Vicki!

Trial, Error, and Success! Bedtime on Their Time

I started thinking: What about handing the whole bedtime routine over to the kids? Are they ready for that? Am I ready for that? What about that first week, when we did Do Nothing, Say Nothing, and they all stayed up late watching TV just because they could? Will they do that every night? Will it drive me crazy? Am I crazy for even considering this?

Vicki's voice was clear in my head: "Give them practice with setting their own bedtime while they're at home. Otherwise, you'll spend thousands of dollars for college and send them off and they'll have *no idea* how to manage this bedtime thing!"

Right. Makes perfect sense. "Girls?" I said, "I'm going to

stop telling you when bedtime is. I want you to have the chance to practice figuring out how much sleep you need to feel good each day and figure out how to get it. And as long as I'm still up, you can get a bedtime visit whenever you choose. Okay?" Half-interested nods all around. They knew we'd been slowly sliding toward this approach for months already.

Still, saying it out loud made me nervous. It helped that J was on board right away. It made sense to him too. I explained the rationale and then shrugged, "I don't know how it'll go, but let's try it."

The result? Quite anticlimactic. Sometimes they stay up late. Sometimes they don't. Sometimes they drag in the morning. Sometimes they don't. We have trial and error and the freedom to learn from it. The other night our six-year-old stayed up too late and only made it as far as my office. When I went to bed she was asleep under my desk. Before this I would have carried her to bed to make sure she got a good night's sleep. No more. Her good night's sleep is up to her now. And at some point during the night she quietly moved to her bed, where I found her in the morning, warm and cozy.

Our evenings are, again, transformed. No more deadline. No more haggling. No more guilt over my own inconsistency. Just trust and calm and space to learn.

Then, the other day, any lingering doubts vanished when I found my nine-year-old's blank Roadmap, which I had printed out for her, had recently been filled in:

Start: "Tired. Bed too late. Waking up too late."

Middle: "Go to bed a little earlier. Set my alarm later."

Finish: "Getting up at 6:30 A.M. Not tired. Find a good time to go to bed by myself."

So, once again, I find myself wondering what I was so worried about.

In Kids I Trust

At least I trust my kids a lot more than I used to. I will continue to nurture that trust. Where does the distrust come from in the first place, I wonder? Society? All that garbage people say? ("They're 'just' kids…Give 'em an inch, they'll take a mile…Kids need tons of reminders…" etc.)

Or is it that, as adults, we forget what it's like to be learning and figuring out the world for the first time? And so when our kids make one mistake, or take several tries to get something right, we assume they can't be trusted.

I'm finding again and again that it's simply not true. But still I have to actively remind myself, even as my girls remind me, over and over again.

Our seven-year-old skipped school yesterday. She woke up an hour late and said, "It's too embarrassing! I'm staying home today." The voice in my head started right away: What will people think? What if she does this again tomorrow? What if she enjoys staying home so much that she never goes to school again?!

Shhhhhhh, I said to the voice. And then I said to her, "Okay. I have to go to work now. I have my cell phone, and you can walk over to Nana and Papa's whenever you'd like." We agreed that TV and computer would be off limits for the day (in big picture terms, no school equals no job equals no money equals no electronics, which they totally get).

"Bye, have a good day," I said, and kissed her forehead. "Bye, Mom," she said softly. She wasn't upset, but I could see and feel her disappointment in herself. No need to rub it in, she was doing that all on her own.

She actually did have a good day, though. She played with the dogs. She did an art project with Nana. And then guess what she did today? She got up extra early and went to school. Go figure.

On top of that, on the way in to school I put on the brakes, gave my ten-year-old a look of concern in the rearview mirror, and said, "Do you know that we're not going home today before the birthday party?" I let the car roll to a stop, fully expecting a panicked response from the backseat. But what I heard instead was, "Oh, yeah, Mom. Here's the present, and I have my homework and my reading log..."

I started the car going again and tried not to look surprised.

Why was I surprised? Why wouldn't she have all her stuff? Like I said—trust. I'll keep working on it.

Respect: We Earn It, Therefore We Enjoy It

You can scare your kids into showing respect for you, but it's not real. It might even make you feel good and powerful and in control. But it's not real respect for you as a parent and as a person. Earning a child's respect takes time, and it takes strength and courage on a parent's part to earn it.

The bonus in doing this is that, as our respect for each other grows, so does the child's respect for himself. Like two flowers drinking from the same trickle of water.

And bonus number two: that mutual respect and self-respect feed directly into the harmony of our home.

For example, last night my six-year-old was hyped-up and determined to drive her sisters batty. Knowing that it was her twelve-year-old sister's turn to be responsible for the state of the living room, she proceeded to pull all the cushions off the couch onto the floor and tipped the coffee table onto its side.

F: Mooooom! Look what she's doing! Are you going to do something about it? Are you going to make her put them back?! No, right? You're not going to do anything because you wouldn't do anything to help your dear daughter! [Said with a scowl.]

Me: I'm supposed to ignore the behavior I don't want. So I don't really know what to do... At family meeting, didn't you guys agree that you could ask each other to clean up any messes that were left in your contribution area?

F: Ask each other? Oh, great. She'll just say no. And then I'll have to do it. I always end up doing her work!

I didn't say anything. I went in the other room and pet the dogs and pondered. What is C trying to get? Attention—whatever kind she can get. What does she really want? Connection. She's trying to connect in inappropriate ways. How can I help? Hmm.

At this point in my parenting journey, all my old lectures, scoldings, and threats have become so faded and foreign that I'm hardly even tempted by them anymore. What a relief. And suddenly it came to me.

"Hey, C!"

"Yeah?"

"Wanna play a game before bedtime?"

"Okay!"

"Would you be willing to put all this back so we can play in here?"

"Okay!"

And then I watched with delight as she immediately went to work wrestling each and every heavy leather cushion back into place. My middle child happened to notice one cushion was backward and silently came over and helped her turn it around. In less than five minutes it was done and we sat down to play our game.

F walked by and said, "Oh, the couch looks all beautiful!"

R-E-S-P-E-C-T. For C, for myself, for F, for our home. Everyone feels good about it. That's how you know it's real.

We Changed Our Thinking and It Changed Our Lives

The best part of this hands-off approach to parenting is that it simply changed our lives. A few lightbulbs went off, and I thought, *No wonder I am so exhausted all the time, I do everything around here!* Our house was a mess this week, but it was so much less stressful. My husband and I realized how controlling we were, how often we said no, how we take the children's independence away, that we demanded respect even though we didn't give it. Vicki's insight and exercises set the stage for my husband and me to have positive dialogue about what was happening with our children and with us. It brought us closer together and helped us to help each other in a positive way, not by nagging or blaming.

One or Two Mistakes Is All It Takes

Vicki's hands-off approach to parenting had been recommended to us by friends and by one of our children's teachers. After a particularly tough morning, leaving the house with two children crying, another unfed, and me on the verge of tears, we decided it was time!

Now we have shifted most of the responsibility of getting out of the house to the kids. They make their lunches the night before. If they choose to dillydally in the morning rather than take care of their responsibilities, they own the consequences. They may be hungry, have no mittens, forget their homework, go to school in jammies, but it only takes one or two times for them to realize that they can make a difference in how their day progresses.

My husband and I make breakfast, drive them to the bus, and give them a kiss goodbye, but the rest is now up to them and, thankfully, they rise to the occasion! If one of them has a rough morning because they chose not to take care of their responsibilities, that one is usually the first one up and ready the following day!

The evening routine is even more predictable and steady. My husband and I do the dinner cleanup while the kids get their evening responsibilities taken care of (jammies, lunches, etc.). When the kitchen is cleaned up, I do cocoa and book reading every night. If they do not have their responsibilities done, they miss out on books and cocoa! Most of the time, that table is filled with chocolate-faced kids enjoying several books, and I am calm and happy and not racing around trying to get lunches made and doing things that the kids can handle for themselves!

I could ramble on for hours about the program's impact on our family. To summarize, it has given us a completely new approach to family dynamics that now incorporates balance, trust, and family values. This acts as an incredible springboard to promote capable, confident, responsible children. It seems like a mouthful, but it is challenging to hit on all the pieces that have had an impact on our family in one sentence.

Our Home Is a Happier Place to Be

I now live by, "a misbehaving child is a discouraged child," a quote by Rudolf Dreikurs that I learned in one of Vicki's classes. I can now usually pinpoint exactly what went wrong right before someone acted out. It is amazing. I feel much more connected to my children, and our home is a happier place to be. And *everyone* is more respectful to each other.

Contributions, Connection, and Confidence

Our kids smile to themselves as their friends' parents are packing and nagging all around them. The contributions have really fueled this. They are invested in meals, enjoy them more, and appreciate what it takes to make it all happen every day. The family joy each day is much greater now that they are participating in all aspects of moving the chains down the field every day.

They have some swagger when they haul tons of wood, move the laundry along, empty the dishwasher without reminding, or get all their gear packed up for a ski trip. They are more courageous and feel so much more capable in everything. Their feelings of being capable transfer to other areas, and they are willing to try more tasks and put themselves out there.

"Feeling connected" is a phrase my kids hear and refer to all the time, too. My oldest even notices that his grandmother needs to see all of us more so she feels connected. This one in particular hits for all of us.

Being more engaged with how my kids feel about their school life, family life, and sports and with their thoughts about the world feels great, rather than being caught up in the reminding and nagging about our to-do lists that disconnect us.

They trust us more, now that we all have a base philosophy. We have more room in our hearts and minds for meaningful connection, rather than thinking we are effective and useful with all our reminding and badgering. They are grateful that we trust them and have risen up with pride to tasks we weren't formerly considering sharing, just because we thought it was easier and more efficient to do some of those things ourselves. We are all more connected in the best kind of ways.

13

Simulating the Real World: Raising the Next Generation of Leaders

Once the family dynamic improves and clearer communication, realistic expectations, and a mutually respectful decision-making process are underway, something magical begins to happen: the effects spill out into the community. Children take their newfound skills, their confident and resilient natures, their ability to deal with frustration, and their practical skills in navigating rough patches, and they unleash them on the world.

They also begin to view people in a different light. They notice strengths, not weaknesses, show appreciation for differences and uniqueness rather than looking for separation, and learn not to take for granted what they appreciate in others. They make efforts to help, to work together, and to participate in the communal running of society. They understand that people are capable of making decisions and begin to trust others with their own responsibilities. They don't blame people for their mistakes and they can independently coexist with whomever they encounter.

As I have said throughout this book, we are raising the next generation of leaders. How they view themselves and others will influence the kind of leaders they become. If they spent their childhoods being micromanaged, controlled, corrected, and punished, it's hard to imagine that they will grow into reflective, kind, firm, creative, and courageous leaders. Here are stories that capture the possibilities that surface when we decide to raise our kids with a more hands-off, relationship-focused approach.

Responsible Behavior

When my daughter started to drive I overheard her and several of her friends talking around our kitchen table:

"We need to make an agreement before we go to the party tonight."

Her friends looked a little baffled but said, "Sure, okay."

"We have to agree that someone will be the designated driver and we have to agree that we have to stay with a buddy and we all have to agree that if one of us wants to go, we all go."

"Why do we have to make an agreement?"

"Because that is what responsible people do and now that we are driving, we have to act like responsible people. If we say we are old enough to drive and go to parties, then we have to be old enough to make decisions that will keep us all safe."

Her friends agreed. They continued the conversation for another ten minutes, talking about the other responsibilities that went along with being new drivers. It was fascinating to listen to how my daughter had taken a standard practice in our family and applied it to her life as a more independent young adult.

This was the first of many conversations and agreements my daughter made with the people in her life.

Common Courtesies

Whenever we go out, whether it's to a restaurant, school function, or the theater, the kids seem to be more aware of the people around them. They can be counted on to hold the door for someone, let someone go ahead of them, help someone in the grocery line, make eye contact, and speak to strangers instead of acting like frightened children.

Problem Solvers

When my son was ten years old, he came home from school one day very upset. He typically came home stressed and upset, but today he was different. There was conviction and passion in his voice when we talked, rather than just frustration.

We had adopted a more hands-off approach to parenting nearly five years earlier and we felt confident that our son had the skills he needed to deal with the ups and down of school.

On this particular day, he told me that he could not go back to school ever again. I asked him why and he said that he was tired of his teacher making fifth and sixth-grade boys cry. He told me that kids should be able to go to school and not have the teacher make them cry.

I listened. I didn't say a word. I knew that if I was quiet, he would eventually come up with an idea that felt "right" to him. I waited. "I got it! I know what I have to do," he said. I smiled. He declared, "I am going to have a family meeting with her. Will you come with me and listen and be my witness, but I will do the talking." I gave him a big hug. He stood up, walked over, picked up a pen and some paper, and began making the agenda for the meeting.

He started with an appreciation for his teacher: *Ms. M., I appreciate that you are a strict teacher and how hard you work to get us ready for seventh grade.* Then asked a question: *Do you have any problems with my behavior in class?* Then he stated his problem: *I have a problem when there is yelling in the classroom and my friends cry. Do you think we could come up with a solution that would work for everyone?* He then called the teacher and asked for a meeting.

On the day of the meeting, I sat in the corner as an observer. He sat across the table from his teacher and read his notes. He was articulate and confident. She listened and was clearly amazed at his ability to communicate. Her reply was that if the class would listen, she would not have to yell, but he at least felt better voicing his concerns.

A few days went by and I checked back with him. He told me that things were a bit better and that even though Ms. Moira did not say she would stop yelling, he thought she was trying. When I asked him how he felt about going to fifth grade now, he said, "I have to go to school, Mom, Ms. Moira needs me."

Note from Vicki: I know this family and have for nearly fifteen years. J had been in trouble at school, beginning in kindergarten until the fourth grade. When his parents finally gave up trying to control him and focused instead on developing a relationship with him, things began to turn around. They spent five years teaching him, supporting him, listening to him, and showing faith in him. In those five years, he developed the confidence in himself to use a skill he learned in his family to solve a problem at school. Can you imagine the kind of man he will be in another ten years? Extraordinary.

Here is a story to illustrate how my own daughter challenged her second-grade teacher, who had a habit of embarrassing students; my daughter felt this was unacceptable behavior for any teacher. She asked for a meeting and articulated her concern and provided three possible solutions. At the end of the year, I got a note from the teacher. It read:

Dear Mrs. H.,
I am a better teacher as a result of your daughter and the courage she found to challenge a person in a position of author-

ity. I only wish my coworkers, who agreed with her assessment of me, had the courage to talk to me years before. I can only imagine the teacher I might have been. I have been teaching for twenty-two years. This was the best year of my career.

Noticing Strengths

Here are just a few of the hundreds of stories I have heard over the years of kids rising to the occasion and acting in extraordinary ways. With the bullying issue at the forefront of our minds, we can see how a school could be influenced for the better when classrooms are full of kids with not only tolerant but generous views of their classmates and the confidence to reach out and make a connection.

Ruby came home from school in kindergarten and exclaimed, "There is a new girl in my class, she does not know anyone, and looked scared. I stayed by her all day. I am going to be her friend."

When Peter was in second grade, we witnessed a mother screaming at her son after he was suspended from school for knocking desks over during class. Peter turned to me and said, "He was mad. Causing trouble is not who he is, Mom. It is just what he did."

When Georgie was in the ninth grade, her guidance counselor called to tell me that there was a boy who had been sitting alone at lunch. Georgie noticed him and decided to sit with him every day after that. Another week passed and a few other kids joined her at the table. When I asked Georgie about it, she said, "Nobody should have to sit by themselves at lunch. He's really funny, if you take a minute to get to know him."

When Bella was in the fourth grade she advocated for a classmate who was being excluded from the group. She would spend time with him each day at recess and offer support and strategies to navigate the harshness of recess that could go along with picking teams for sports. When I asked her about it, she told me, "If kids would just stop focusing on what they don't like about other kids, and take time to notice something they do like, everybody could be friends."

Kindness and Compassion

We started family meetings, which included appreciations, when my kids were five and three years old, in utero, and a twinkle in our eyes. I now live with four kids, ages sixteen, fourteen, ten, and seven. We have gone through years of practice; many a family meeting ended with tears of frustration, though even more ended in tears of joy. In these instances it is the appreciations that always drop us to our knees.

Appreciations are powerful. Not only do they remind us each week how amazing we are as individuals and how we have impacted the lives of our family members, they shift the focus of the family and each individual in the family from finding problems and complaining to noticing what is good about people.

As a result, I hear several times a year from teachers, coaches, the parents of our kids' friends, and family members that I have some of the kindest, most compassionate, and most inclusive kids they have ever met. It isn't by accident. We practice.

Kicked Out of the Club

There is a price to all this new parenting. I've discovered that I'm out of the club. The stressed-out, at-the-end-of-their-rope parent's club. I used to bond with people over that. We'd exchange horror stories and roll our eyes together and shake our heads about how our kids were clearly on a mission to drive us crazy. I still listen to people's horror stories, but I find myself just nodding and smiling and saying things like, "Yeah, that's hard...I know what you mean."

And I do know what they mean. It is hard. Really hard, when you're trying to make it work with old thinking—without new information, new life-changing information.

Miles of Smiles

Two boys buy donuts unattended while the staff looks on adoringly at these two problem solvers who can *barely* see over the counter to the donut display.

I watch and smile.

Four-year-old asks, "Can I get a donut?"

I reply, "Did you bring your wallet?"

He answers, "Yeah."

I say, "Then sure, get a donut."

Brother says, "I didn't bring mine!"

Four-year-old says, "I'll buy yours if you pay me back."

They both agree, "Deal."

Brotherly Love

One day, as I was picking the boys up from school, a teacher pulled me aside to share the following. "Hey, I just have to tell you. Every day, T comes to pick N up after school. He's such a good brother. They have little disputes, like today, about whether or not you're picking them up or they're walking home. I just crack up listening to them work it out. I only hope my two kids, now three and one year old, get along and communicate like these two!"

Patience

I remember we were in the store and it was a holiday and there was holiday candy everywhere and N, who was four years old, said, "I want this candy."

I said, "Did you bring your wallet?"

He said, "Well, no."

I said, "Okay, bring it next time."

He said, "Oh yeah, I will."

Not five seconds later the woman in the aisle turned and said, "Wow, that was impressive."

Money Management 101

We were leaving Walmart. A girl stopped and asked for four dollars.

I stuttered, "Well…um…"

From the backseat my seven-year-old son said, "I have four dollars!"

I said, "Okay then."

He took out his wallet and gave her the money. She thanked him. As we drove off, he said, "I hope she really does need that money to buy vitamins. If she does, that will really help. If she doesn't, well, I guess I wasted four dollars." Then we went on to chat about if she's lying, it's like the boy who cried wolf, and someday when she really does need money, nobody will give it to her. Then we moved on. He felt good helping her and was okay with the risk.

A Natural Life Lesson

We had a huge cash pile in the family meeting box. My son decided to use it to purchase a video game from our neighbor.

When we showed up to family meeting and people only got half of their regular allowance because there was no cash left, man, his brothers let him know how uncool that was. He went back, returned the game, got the cash, and paid the family back. If I had made some big stealing ordeal of it, it would've been a guilty mess. But I realized it seemed reasonable for him, at six years old; never having done anything like this before, he thought it was a good way to get what he wanted. But then, upon facing the family, he knew it was a lapse in judgment. Without moralizing it overtly, he learned that being dishonest wasn't in his best interest. He learned and I barely said anything about it.

AFTERWORD

Ode to Mom and Dad:
The Kids' Perspective

I am often asked what my children think about being raised by parents who took a hands-off approach to parenting. Now that they are out of the house and on their own, and have had some time to reflect, I asked each of them to share one aspect of our family that impacted their life and is still impacting it today.

Hannah, Twenty-Three Years Old: Confidence and Trust

Maybe the most important thing my parents ever taught me was to have confidence in myself and to trust myself in every aspect of my life. But you don't build confidence and learn to trust yourself unless a parent has confidence and trust in you first.

I can remember my school morning routine as if it were yesterday. As a five-year-old kindergartner, living in Edmonds, Washington, I would get up to my alarm clock at six in the morning every day. My first stop was to my parents' room to say good morning and give them kisses. Then I would head to the kitchen and make myself a bowl of cereal (which I had set out the night before). I would eat, pack my lunch, and brush my teeth and get dressed. How is it that a five-year-old can do so much on her own? It's not so hard with practice and support from parents who are confident that, with a bit of training and lots of encouragement, any five-year-old can handle a morning routine. And, truth be told, a mom who was willing to admit that if she was in the kitchen with me, she would find a way to "tweak" my routine and throw me off my game, so she stayed out of the kitchen until I was ready. She had her coffee in her room and waited for me to come and get her. Talk about a parent who trusts her child.

Mom worked from home running a small childcare center. I took the bus to school and, when I was ready, Mom would put on her slippers and walk me to the end of the driveway, where we would wait for the bus together. This was my favorite part of the day; I got a solid ten minutes of Mommy and me time. We got to talk about anything I wanted and as the bus drove up I would kiss her goodbye and head to school. Now, I know you must be thinking, Well, why didn't she just let you walk to the end of the driveway by yourself if she trusted you could do it? It wasn't that she didn't trust me, she walked me to the end of the driveway and waited with me because she knew how much I loved this time with her. I looked forward to these ten minutes and I knew that if I wanted that time with her, I would have to manage my mornings. I loved the feeling of independence and I loved the time with Mom. It was a win/win from my five-year-old perspective

As I grew up, I added more responsibilities to my plate, including showering in the morning, helping Mom get Zoe and Brady ready for school, doing my dishes after breakfast, and picking up my room before school. When our family grew and became the Hofenways (a combination of two last names), my responsibilities grew, along with the confidence and trust I felt my parents had in me and that I had in myself. I was mowing the lawn, bringing the trash and recycling to the corner, shoveling snow, starting the cars, and helping with the weekly menu by the time I was twelve. These responsibilities continued to grow over the years, as did my sense of confidence.

One of the ways my parents sent that message that they had confidence in me was to teach my siblings and me how to make important phone calls. At fourteen years old I was calling to make doctors' appointments and check out movie times, and I even helped my mom in her business, making phone calls to customers. Talk about feeling important and valuable. The confidence I felt played a part in my ability to fill out job applications, make lists of questions to ask my potential employer, remember to ask for their name on the phone, and nail down details if there was the possibility of an interview. When I was asked to come in for an interview I felt confident making eye contact, shaking hands firmly, and asking questions most kids my age had never even considered asking a potential employer. I was often hired after my first interview and I am sure that it was the result of the confidence I exuded. I can't tell you how great it feels for a fourteen-year-old to know that she can land a job on her own, with no "help" from her parents. Knowing that I could make my own money and would be able to support myself when I left home fed my feelings of confidence and this gave me more courage to do more in my life.

It seems like such a small thing, teaching your kids how to make their lunch, get up with an alarm clock, set their own morning routine, but the result is a twenty-three-year-old who feels empowered in her life and confident about the decisions she makes, and knows with certainty that her parents have faith in her abilities.

Colin, Twenty Years Old: The Power of the Tribe

I didn't pay much attention to the way people described my family until I heard the word "tribe," and I knew the word was perfect for what the seven of us created together.

In high school, if you played sports you had to sign a non-negotiable agreement: no partying, no use of inappropriate or offensive language, maintain a GPA of 2.5 or higher, and so on. The equivalent of that nonnegotiable agreement in our family was that you are either part of the tribe or you are not. It was as simple as that.

Being part of the tribe meant bringing your very best to every conversation, every discussion, and every disagreement we had. My parents cared about our perspective, our opinions, our preferences, and our ideas for solutions. They made it clear that without each of our contributions to the health of the family, the family would suffer. The message was clear; we are in this together. What affects one of us affects all of us. Becoming a member of this tribe wasn't a matter of clicking a button or writing a $200.00 check to cover the membership initiation fee. The only currency we worked with was love, sweat, and tears.

I've heard my friends comment that it was clear to them when they visited me at home that we had something special, something unique. I never realized it, but I feel our family, above all else, values each other and the relationships that make up our family. These relationships are the most important part of my life.

Being born into the tribe also has its responsibilities. You were expected to pull your weight around the house, keep it company clean, as my mom liked to say. We all chipped in, every day. We created routines that kept the family running smoothly, and these routines, whether we knew it or not, became like second nature to all of us and kept the family in a "flow." There weren't many arguments about who was supposed to do what, and by the time we were all teens, menial household chores and other responsibilities were considered part of life.

When something so basic as the functionality of a household begins to self-propel, you stop noticing the small things your siblings do that make you a little crazy. Instead, you learn to admire, to appreciate, and to love each member of your family, and the best part is, you know they love you in the same way.

Those of us who drove were willing to pick up a sibling if they were stranded at school, a sporting event, the movies, or a school dance or take them to an early-morning swim practice. We depended on each other and we worked as a team. I know I never considered what we did as anything other than normal until I heard my friends talk about how rare this was in other families.

It isn't until you can truly value what the people around you are bringing to the table, as well as express this to them, that you can say, I have found my tribe, I have found my home. I have found my home and it is in the hearts of my family.

Zoe, Twenty Years Old: Family Meetings Rock

What's one word to describe growing up in a household of seven? Chaos! It's the first word that comes into most people's minds when I say I am one of five kids, and, truthfully, sometimes it pops into mine. But life wasn't chaotic. It was calm and organized and, well, it was fun.

Weekly family meetings were the one aspect of our lives that kept us all grounded and running like a well-oiled machine. Before we were even remotely close to grasping the idea of what an "appreciation" was or that helping Mom unload the dishwasher was actually called a chore, we were sitting in our high chairs partaking of the family meeting.

As we grew older and things like ballet class, karate lessons, gymnastics, swim team, yearbook, sleepovers, lacrosse, and just about every other activity one could cram into a day, took over our lives, family meetings became that much more essential. Today, I am able to schedule and manage my time efficiently and to prioritize what I want to do with my days, my weeks, and even what I want to get out of my year here at school.

Appreciations given each week, to the person on your right, the person on your left, or to every single member of the family, reminded each of us just how important we were to each other. It helped us see the best in each other and to point out strengths instead of what someone did that drove you crazy. There wasn't much squabbling among the five of us kids, and I think that's because every week we were giving and getting appreciations. As a freshman in college this year, I have experienced firsthand just how hurtful and cruel people can be to each other, and I owe appreciations a big thank-you for helping me be a more thoughtful and kind person.

Distributing contributions was a chance to barter with a sibling and convince someone to change chores with you. We learned to negotiate, compromise, and cooperate, and we understood that if we didn't each do our part each week, the family would suffer. Whether I was out on a trail during an Outward Bound experience or traveling in Argentina or volunteering in Ecuador, I felt confident that I could do what was necessary to ensure I had an awesome trip. I knew how to do my own laundry, buy and cook my own food, find bus routes, talk to locals, ask for directions, book flights, and immerse myself in the culture instead of worrying about how to take care of myself. Living in hostels also made me realize that being self-reliant made my experience so much more enjoyable. I saw a lot of kids my age who were totally overwhelmed with everything they had to do just to get around in a new country.

Getting our weekly allowance was a chance to replenish our wallets (the allowance was only given out until we were fourteen and able to make our own money) and learn to manage our money beginning at the age of three. Don't even get me started on how this has helped me in my life as a kid who loves to travel abroad and go on adventures, and who is living three thousand miles away from home attending college and working. Money is no problem for me. I understand how to budget, I understand how to save, and I even understand that sometimes I have to blow a bit on myself (this is hard for me to do and my mom has to encourage me to treat myself). As I watch other people my age I am so thankful that my parents put those silvery coins in my hand and gave me time to practice figuring out how to manage my money before I was out on my own.

Family meetings reminded all of us, each of us, of who we really were. As we grew older, you might find one of us rolling our eyes or saying something snarky under our breaths about family meetings, but had family meetings not been a part of our lives we would not be the successful, loving, independent, generous, forgiving, kind, thoughtful, hard-working adults we are today.

To conclude, it's only right that I end with an infamous appreciation. I appreciate my family: Vicki, Iain, Hannah, Colin, Kiera, and Brady for allowing and helping me become the mature, loud, outgoing, sarcastic, affectionate, driven, adventurous freshman that I am today.

Kiera, Nineteen Years Old: Independence

By the time I headed into kindergarten I was able to get up on my own, pack my own lunch, and make sure I had all my gear for school. My parents raised me with the notion that if I wasn't going to make my own lunch, who would? Packing my own lunch at the age of five put me ahead of my classmates in terms of self-reliance. When I was in the first grade, my parents taught me how to manage my own money using a weekly allowance, while my classmates "borrowed" money from their parents every time they wanted something of their own. In the second grade I was figuring out ways to get home from gymnastics when both my parents were busy.

These baby steps toward independence eventually gave me the confidence to attend an Outward Bound Program for two weeks in the eighth grade; spend a semester in Spain during my junior year of high school; spend four weeks between my junior and senior years attending the Governer's Institute of the Arts; travel to Argentina for two weeks to visit and travel with my sister; and to apply to colleges three thousand miles from home.

Having just completed an incredible first semester of college at Chapman University in Orange, California, I am so thankful my parents were committed to raising five independent kids. As a freshman, I found myself surrounded by eighteen-, nineteen-, even twenty-year-old Chapman students asking me how to operate a washing machine or sharing that they had never cleaned a bathroom in their entire lives! Keep in mind that these students were some of the brightest kids in their high school class, maintaining at least a 3.5 GPA to even be considered by Chapman. I was blown away. One student even asked me why I was paying my monthly phone bill. "Don't your parents pay it for you?" she asked. "Uh, no. No, they don't." It crossed my mind that, for many of my classmates, this was their first experience of real independence, having been completely dependent on their parents for the past twenty years of their lives.

Sometimes you realize just how lucky you are only when

you see yourself in comparison to others. This sense of independence and curiosity I have about the world and all it has to offer started when I made that first sandwich as a five-year-old. I haven't looked back once.

Brady, Nineteen Years Old: Trust

When I was growing up there were many things my parents taught me, beginning at a very young age. Being responsible for myself and for my decisions is among them. I was responsible for getting dressed, cleaning up, making my own lunches, and, in general, taking care of myself from the time I was in the first grade. In addition to taking care of ourselves, everyone in the household contributed to cleaning and to the upkeep of the house. All of the kids would choose a weekly chore, which included cleaning the kitchen, vacuuming, bringing in wood, cleaning bathrooms, taking care of animals, and other tasks around the house. Because of how early I learned these skills, by the time I reached middle school they were second nature and a habit to me. I considered myself a responsible person.

But the most important lessons I learned were about earning the trust of someone you respect, the responsibilities associated with that trust, and how difficult it can be to regain it once that trust is broken. In this area, I had much growing to do. Each time I set out on a new experience, I could feel my parents' belief in my abilities and their trust that no matter what happened, I could handle the outcome.

There were many times, when I was young, that my parents put their trust and faith in me, confident that I would make the most of the opportunities placed in front of me; and time and time again I failed to appreciate and take advantage of many of these opportunities. There are countless instances, both small and large, that display just how deeply my parents trusted me and, instead of making me feel bad when I messed up, allowed me to gather information about myself and the experience and use it to grow and mature.

One glaring example of their trust was the year I spent in Pennsylvania at a private school called Westtown. I had convinced my parents that if given a chance to attend a challenging private school that cared more about learning than about test taking and homework, I would excel in school. The tuition was, as one can imagine, pretty steep, and there was an understanding at the beginning of the year that I would achieve high enough grades to get grants and scholarships to help with the costs of attending for the following years. I admit that I was capable of achieving these grades, so their expectations were not unreasonable.

Instead of taking advantage of the opportunities being afforded me of attending four years at a top boarding school, I proceeded to get average grades and worry more about what everyone thought of me than what I had to do to get the better education I said I wanted. After just one year, I returned home with nothing to show but a few new experiences, a few new friends, and a large amount of money wasted on nothing. However, the experience showed me that I was looking for more than a traditional education could offer—without the opportunity to try something and not accomplish the expected results, I would not have had the awareness about myself that I gained from that year away.

After that experience, it's easy to understand why my parents might not have trusted me with another big decision that required a commitment on my part. And for a while they seemed hesitant, and that is understandable given the magnitude of the trust I had just broken.

But it was barely a year later when they trusted me with an even bigger decision, one that would impact the rest of my life.

This time I was asking them to let me drop out of high school, get my GED, and spend three months in Nepal. And this time I was determined to restore their trust in my decision-making abilities.

I took care of everything. I made appointments with guidance counselors, filled out paperwork, spoke to teachers, answered questions, and stated my case to the administration of my high school. I signed up to take the GED, passed it, and prepared myself for the trip. I filled out applications, wrote family and friends for recommendations, spoke to officials at the organization hosting the trip. I made lists of the supplies I would need, how much money I would need, the immunizations that were required, and anything else having to do with traveling abroad for three months in Nepal. My parents watched as I regained their trust and proved to them and to myself that I could be responsible for this life decision. They showed their trust in me by making another sizable investment in my "education."

Soon, I found myself halfway around the world in a completely new land. In what felt like both the longest and the shortest three months of my life, I learned more about the world and myself than I possibly could have in any high school.

Without my parents' unwavering trust in me, the amazing experience I had in Nepal never would have happened. The growth I experienced would not have happened.

The lesson at the end of the day is to teach your children as much as you can and trust that they will learn, but never forget that there are some lessons that kids must learn on their own. A parent's job is to give kids the tools they need to learn those lessons as quickly and smoothly as possible. And trusting that your kids will learn those lessons makes all the difference.

RESOURCES

Adler, Alfred. *What Life Could Mean to You*. New York: Oneworld Publications, 1992.

Adler, Alfred. *The Pattern of Life*. New York: Adler School of Professional Psychology, Inc., 1996.

Bettner, Betty Lou. *An Adlerian Resource Book: A Sampler of Reproducible Educational Materials*. Chicago: North American Society of Adlerian Psychology, 1989.

Bettner, Betty Lou and Amy Lew. *Raising Kids Who Can*. Newton, MA: Connexions Press, 2005.

Covey, Stephen R. *The 7 Habits of Highly Effective People*. New York: Simon and Schuster/Fireside, 1989.

Dinkmeyer, Don, and Rudolf Dreikurs. *Encouraging Children to Learn*. New York: Hawthorn Books, 1963.

Dinkmeyer, Don, and Gary McKay. *Systematic Training for Effective Parenting*. Circle Pines, MN: American Guidance Service, 1997.

Dewey, Edith. *Basic Applications of Adlerian Psychology*. Florida: CMTI Press, 1991.

Dreikurs, Rudolf, and v. Soltz. *Children: The Challenge*. New York: Hawthorn Books, 1964.

Dreikurs, Rudolf, B. Grunwald, and F. Pepper. *Maintaining Sanity in the Classroom*. New York: Harper & Row, 1971.

Dreikurs, Rudolf. *Social Equality: The Challenge of Today*. Chicago: Alfred Adler Institute of Chicago, 1971.

Dreikurs, Rudolf, and Margaret Goldman. *The ABCs of Guiding the Child*. Chicago: Alfred Adler Institute of Chicago, 1990.

Dreikurs, Rudolf, and Loren Grey. *The New Approach to Discipline: Logical Consequences*. New York: Penguin Group, 1993.

Evans, Tim, PhD. *The Art of Encouragement: Human Relations Training*. Athens, Georgia: University of Georgia, Department of Continuing Education, 1989.

Faber, Adele, and Elaine Mazlish. *How to Talk So Kids Will Listen and Listen So Kids Will Talk*. New York: Avon Books, 1990.

Glenn, H.S. and J. Nelsen. *Raising Self-Reliant Children in a Self-Indulgent World*. Rocklin, CA: Prima Publishing & Communications, 1988.

Kurcinka, Mary Sheedy. *Raising Your Spirited Child*. New York: HarperCollins Publishers, 1991.

Kohn, Alfie. *No Contest*. Boston: Houghton Mifflin, 1986.

Lew, Amy and Betty Lou Bettner. *A Parents Guide to Understanding and Motivating Children*. Newton, MA: Connexions Press, 2010.

Main, Frank. *Perfect Parenting and Other Myths*. Minneapolis: CompCare Publishing, 1986.

Manaster, Guy, Genevieve Painter, Danica Deutsch, and Betty Jane Overhold. *Alfred Adler: As We Remember Him*. Chicago: North American Society of Adlerian Psychology, 1977.

Nelsen, Jane. *Positive Discipline*. New York: Random House Publishing Group, 1996.

Popkin, Michael. *Active Parenting*. Atlanta: Active Parenting, 1983.

Walton, Francis X. *Winning Teenagers Over*. Columbia, SC: Adlerian Child Care Books, 1980.

INDEX

ABOUT THE AUTHOR

Vicki Hoefle is a professional parent educator and the creator of the Parenting On Track™ Program. Vicki Hoefle began teaching more than twenty years ago, while running a daycare center in Seattle, Washington. Parents applauded her approach with their children, and wanted to bring her tools and understanding of children home with them. After years of study and everyday practice, Vicki developed the Parenting On Track™ Program, which combines her expertise in Adlerian Psychology and as an ICF certified coach with a suite of time-tested tools. Vicki can speak first-hand to the real world implementation of these strategies with her own family of five children. For more than two decades, Vicki has shared her parenting tips and techniques with families across the country. Her informative and highly engaging presentation style keeps her in demand as a speaker, facilitator, and educator. To learn more about Vicki Hoefle and her program visit www.vickihoefle.com and www.parentingontrack.com